The C Library

The C Library

Kris Jamsa

Osborne **McGraw-Hill**
Berkeley, California

Published by
Osborne **McGraw-Hill**
2600 Tenth Street
Berkeley, California 94710
U.S.A.

For information on translations and book
distributors outside of the U.S.A., please write to
Osborne/McGraw-Hill at the above address.

MS-DOS is a registered trademark of Microsoft Corporation
UNIX is a trademark of Bell Laboratories.

THE C LIBRARY

234567890 DODO 898765

ISBN   0-07-881110-4

Jon Erickson, Acquisitions Editor
Raymond Lauzzana, Technical Editor
Fran Haselsteiner, Copy Editor
Deborah Wilson, Composition
Jan Benes, Text Design
Yashi Okita, Cover Design

Contents

Introduction

Every day each of us uses a device of some type to make life easier. Man has always been a toolmaker, and the computer may very likely become man's most powerful tool. Whether we are fixing a car or appending one file to another, a tool is something that makes our job easier. The purpose of this text is to provide several tools that you can use in the development of C programs.

Over the past few years, the C programming language has grown a great deal in popularity. Although C was originally developed as a systems programming language, the attributes that make C desirable for systems programs are causing many programmers to realize C's potential in many general-purpose applications. These attributes include portability, modifiability, and access to operations that are normally confined to assembly language programming.

In the past, when we wanted to take a program that was written and running on one type of computer and then move it to a different type of computer, a great deal of the program had to be rewritten. A major design goal for the implementation of C was to break through this machine dependence. Because of this, C became one of the most portable languages in existence today. A program written in C for one type of computer, such as the IBM PC, will normally run on a second type of computer, such as an APPLE, with little or no modification.

One goal of any programmer is to break a large task into several smaller and more easily implemented tasks. Many programs that at first appear to be large unsolvable tasks can often be broken down into several smaller subtasks that are easier to design and code. Another major advantage of breaking a program into several functions is that the functions created for one program can often be used again in an unrelated application with little or no modification. If we implement most of our program with functions, we increase the readability of the code and decrease the development and testing time of the program. In addition, we create a series of routines that can be placed into a library and shared by other programs. Our goal is to develop functions that perform only one task. In so doing, we will increase the reuseability of our routines.

A Word on UNIX

In the early seventies, Bell Laboratories introduced the UNIX operating system. Because of its tremendous flexibility and the development tools it provides to the user, UNIX has increased in popularity over the past decade. UNIX is well on its way to becoming the industry-wide standard operating system, and because most code used in the UNIX operating system is written in C, the number of applications developed in C and the demand for C programmers will increase for some time to come.

How to Use This Book

This text assumes that you are already familiar with or in the process of learning C. While Chapter 1 provides a brief language overview, it is not intended to be a tutorial on the C programming language. If you are just learning C, many of the routines provided in this text can be used just as they are written to help you develop powerful programs in minimal time. In addition, by examining the routines along with the documentation provided, you will learn a lot more. If you are an advanced C programmer, many of the routines in this text will introduce you to the concepts employed in creating good programming tools, along with an appreciation of the considerations required to develop utility programs similar to those supported by the UNIX operating system. If you are not currently running under UNIX, you can create an environment similar to UNIX by implementing the routines provided at the end of this text.

The most powerful tool at your disposal is the debug write statement. While the routines provided in this text include detailed explanations, the only way to thoroughly understand a routine is to use it. I strongly recommend that you use debug write statements within each routine to increase your understanding of the processing.

Each chapter of this text will introduce a new topic and build upon concepts previously introduced in the text. Chapter 1 provides a brief overview of the C programming language. It is not intended as a tutorial on C but as a quick reference guide. Chapter 2 introduces constants and macros. The constants and macros provided in this chapter are used by the routines in the later chapters and have been placed in the files **defn.h**, **math.h**, and **strings.h**, which should be included in all programs that access the constants or macros. The content of each of these files is provided in Chapter 2. Chapter 3 provides several string manipulation routines. Chapter 4 examines pointers and their use in string manipulation. Chapter 5 centers upon the user interface and the development of good I/O routines. Chapter 6 presents several array manipulation routines that are developed for the generic **array_type**, which allows each routine to be used for applications requiring arrays of **int, float,** or **double.** Chapter 7 examines recursion and how it can be used to simplify difficult programming tasks. Each recursive routine is explained in great detail. Chapter 8 introduces sorting—in particular, the bubble, Shell, and quick sort algorithms. Again, the routines have been developed in a generic manner that allows arrays of type **int, float,** or **double;** in addition, a change in the sorting order (ascending or descending) does not require duplicate routines. Chapter 9 provides a series of routines that perform the trigonometric functions and character conversion. In Chapter 10 we will demonstrate the tools developed in Chapters 2 through 9 as we introduce a series of file manipulation routines that are similar to the utilities provided in a

UNIX environment. Chapter 11 introduces the UNIX pipe and how to develop routines to support it.

The additional effort you spend now developing routines that can be shared by other programs will save you many times the time and effort in the future.

Routines included in this book, as well as other useful routines, are available from the author for $29.95, plus $2.50 shipping and handling. The routines are provided on a 5 1/4-inch floppy disk in MS-DOS format. For McIntosh programmers the routines are available on 3-1/2 inch diskettes for $39.95 plus $2.50 shipping and handling. Write to:

> Kris Jamsa Software, Inc.
> Box 26031
> Las Vegas, NV 89126

C H A P T E R

Language Overview

This chapter is intended to serve as a quick reference as you examine the routines presented in the remainder of the book. In addition to providing a language overview, this chapter introduces syntax charts, their interpretation, and their use in developing programs in C. Don't worry if you are not familiar with syntax charts: by the end of this chapter you should appreciate the level of information provided in a syntax chart, along with the simplicity of its interpretation.

Pointers and Addresses

Most of the routines provided in this text will utilize *pointers* to memory locations. Many programmers have a difficult time with pointers for several reasons. First, some programming languages do not allow the use of pointers. Second, many programmers avoid using pointers since they do not feel comfortable with their manipulation, which only serves to compound the problem. Third, most texts do not explain pointers adequately. Therefore, before addressing the use of pointers in C, let's take a few steps back and review several concepts that are crucial to understanding pointers.

The basic purpose of pointers is to identify memory locations. Since memory is divided into many locations, each of which is capable of storing information, you need a method of placing a value into a specific location in memory and later retrieving the value. The way this is done is by assigning each memory location a unique address. If, for example, you place a value into the memory location whose address is 1000, you can later retrieve the data since you know where it is located. However, if you had to keep track of memory locations by their actual addresses, your programs would be difficult if not impossible to understand. Instead, programming languages allow you to store data in *variables*. A variable can be viewed as nothing more than a meaningful name you assign to a location or series of locations in memory. A variable, therefore, has two values associated with it. The first is the value you assign to the variable. The second is the address, or memory location, the value is contained in.

A pointer is a variable that contains a memory address. In C you use the symbols **&** and * when utilizing pointers. The ampersand (**&**) is used to specify *the address of a variable*, not the value it contains. For example, if you have previously declared the variable **my**—**data** as type int and the pointer **int**—**pointer**, you can assign **int**—**pointer** the address of the variable **my**—**data** in memory as follows:

```
int my_data;          /* declare the variable */
int *int_pointer;     /* declare the pointer   */
int_pointer = &my_data; /* assign the address   */
```

Once **int**—**pointer** is assigned the address of **my**—**data**, both variables reference the same location memory. The asterisk (*) is used to retrieve *the value contained at the location referenced by a pointer*. The expression ***int**—**pointer** references the value contained at the address contained in **int**—**pointer**.

If you have declared the pointer **string** as a pointer to the string "**Computer**", the actual value contained in the variable, **string**, is the address of the first character in the string (**C**). If you print the value contained in **string**, the address of the letter C in memory will be displayed. If you want to print the actual letter, you must use the asterisk as follows:

```
putchar(*string);
```

If you want to print the entire string, you can print the character contained at the location contained in the variable **string** and then increment the value in **string** so that it points to the next character as follows:

```
while (*string != '\0')
  putchar(*string++);
```

The postfix expression ***string++** writes the character contained in the memory location referenced by **string**, and then increments **string** to point to the next location in memory.

The best way to understand pointers is to use them. Chapter 4 presents several routines that utilize pointers to character strings. Experiment with these routines and see if you get the results you anticipated. The use of debug write statements within each of these routines is strongly recommended. If you print the address contained in the pointer, along with the value it references, pointer manipulation should become much more understandable.

Syntax Charts

Before you examine the syntax charts, you should become familiar with the following words:

An *expression* is a symbol or series of symbols that expresses a mathematical operation. The following are valid expressions in C:

$$a = b + 1$$

a   is the same as the expression $a = a + 0$
                           or $a = a - 0$

a++ <= 17

An *identifier* is a unique name that identifies an object. A variable name is an example of an identifier.

A *literal* is a constant value. In the syntax charts later in this chapter, literals are normally the reserved words and punctuation that appear in C.

Syntax charts are read from left to right, in the direction of the arrows that connect the symbols contained in the chart. Since syntax charts are composed of symbols, you can normally understand the syntax charts of a language although you may have never programmed in it. Many experienced computer scientists use syntax charts rather than trying to memorize the syntax for the constructs they don't use on a day-to-day basis. Unfortunately, most of us are never properly introduced to syntax charts. Once you understand the flow of a syntax chart, it provides a very useful tool.

The symbols in Table 1-1 are used in C syntax charts.

Consider the following example:

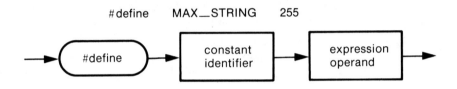

If you start with the first item in the syntax chart and follow the direction of the arrows, the syntax chart provides the following information:

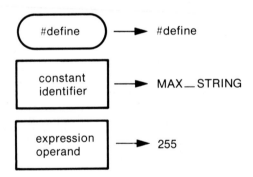

The first two symbols in the chart are fairly straightforward. The third symbol, **expression operand**, requires additional explanation. The rectangle surrounding the words **expression operand** informs you that **expression operand** is defined in terms of another

Table 1-1. Symbols Used in Syntax Charts

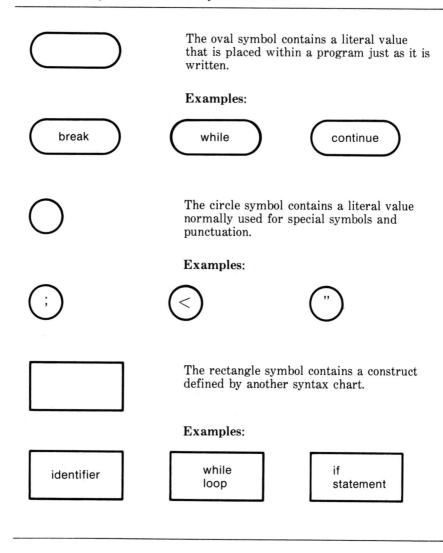

The oval symbol contains a literal value that is placed within a program just as it is written.

Examples:

The circle symbol contains a literal value normally used for special symbols and punctuation.

Examples:

The rectangle symbol contains a construct defined by another syntax chart.

Examples:

syntax chart. If you examine the syntax chart for an expression operand, you will find that it can be any one of the following:

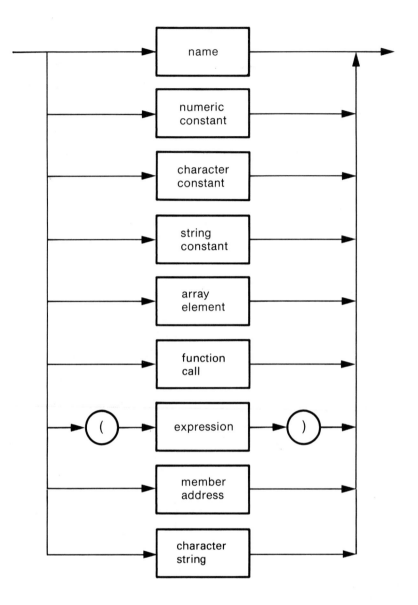

In this case the **expression operand** is the **numeric constant** 255. Consider the following while loop:

```
while (i <= 10)
   i++;
```

If you examine the syntax chart for the while loop,

the literals **while**, **(**, and **)** are again straightforward. The expression in this case is **i** <= 10 and the statement is **i++;**.

If the syntax chart contains more than one possible path, you must select the appropriate path and continue to follow the direction of the arrows. For example, if you want to include the file **stdio.h**, the syntax chart for the **#include** statement provides the following information:

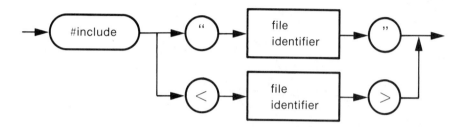

If you already know how the operating system treats files contained with quotes and brackets <>, the syntax chart will provide the correct syntax; otherwise you must examine the reference guide that accompanied your compiler.

The syntax chart is only meant as a guide to the correct syntax of instructions. If you have never worked with syntax charts before, they may at first be intimidating, but keep in mind that the charts are meant to be a tool. Compare the various constructs provided in C (while, do-while, for, if, and so on) to their representations in syntax charts, and you should begin to understand the flow of the charts. If you don't understand a particular chart (a do-while loop, for example), try implementing one in C and then comparing your implementation to the chart. It is important that you become familiar with syntax charts because their popularity is continuing to grow each day.

The following syntax charts illustrate the syntax associated with the C programming language*. Programming examples follow most of the diagrams. Several of the charts are intended for advanced C programmers.

*Brian W. Kernigan and Dennis Ritchie, *The C Programming Language*, Prentice Hall, Inc., Englewood Cliffs, N.J., 1978, Appendix A.

Actual Parameters

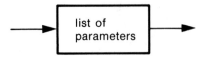

Examples:

a, b, c

c

Arithmetic Operator

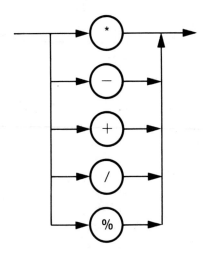

Examples:

x = 3 * 5 − 2;

y = 7/2;

remainder = 3% 2; /* assigns remainder */

Array Element

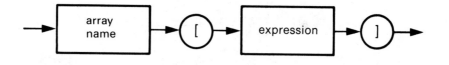

Examples:
string [1];
argv [2];
argv [argc−1];

Array Name

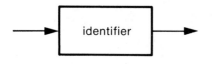

Example:
string

Assignment Operator

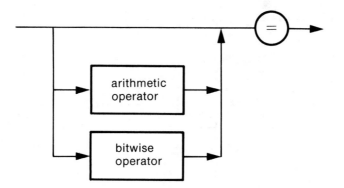

Examples:
x = 5;
x += 5;   /* x = x + 5 */
x >>=2;   /* x = x >>2 */

Binary Operator

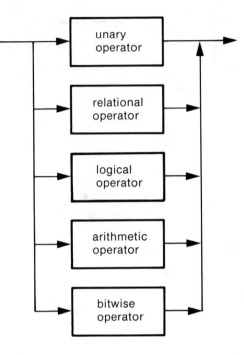

Bitwise Operator

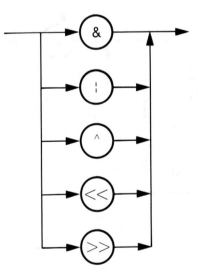

Examples:

```
mask = x & 255;

while (x < 32)
    {
    printf ("%d \n",x);
    x = x<<1;
    }
```

Break Statement

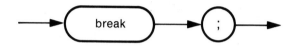

Example:

```
case 2: {
        printf ("The value is 2 \n");
        break;
        }
```

Compound Statement

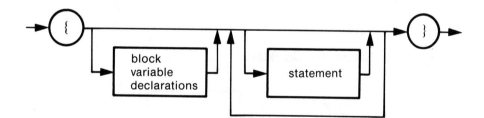

Example:

```
{
 char letter; / * block variable * /
 for (letter = 'a'; letter <= 'z'; letter ++)
   putchar (letter);
 putchar (' \n');
}
```

Case Statement

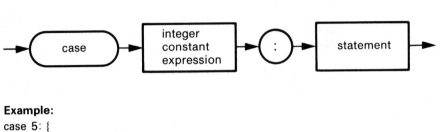

Example:
```
case 5: {
        printf("The digit is 5 \n");
        break;
      }
```

Cast

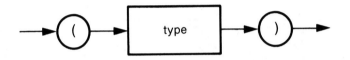

Examples:
```
int i;
float x = 3.775;
i = (int) x;          /* assigns i the value 3 */
i = (int) (x + 0.5);/* assigns i the value 4 */
```

Character Constant

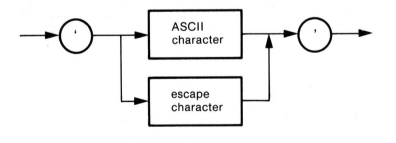

Examples:
```
'A'
'\0'
```

Continue Statement

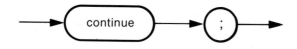

Example:
```
if (i % 2==0)
   continue;
```

Command Line Declarations

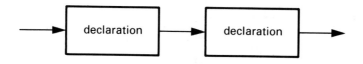

Example:
```
int argc;
char *argv[];
```

Command Line Parameters

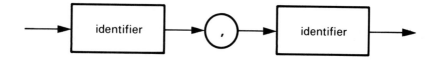

Example:
```
argc, argv
```

Comment

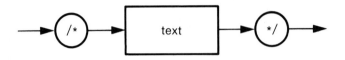

Examples:

/* Stdio.h is included for file manipulation */
/* Comments can
   exceed one line */

Constant

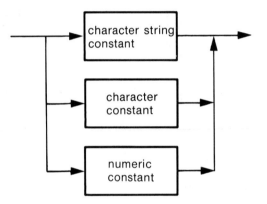

Examples:

"This is a string constant"
'\0'
255

Constant Declaration

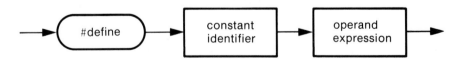

Examples:

#define EOF −1
#define string "This is a string constant"
#define EOL '\n'

Constant Identifier

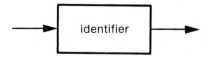

Examples:
NULL
EOF

Declaration

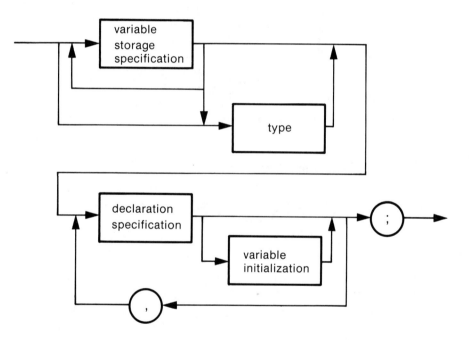

Examples:
static long int count;
long index;
int scores [NUM__SCORES];
float x=3.1573;
int sum, average, max, min;

Declaration Specification

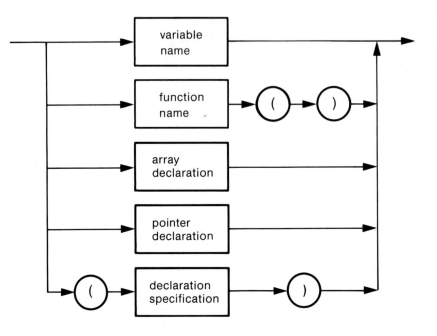

Decrement Operator

Example:
```
for (i = 10; i >= 0; i--)
    printf ("%d \n", i);
```

Default Statement

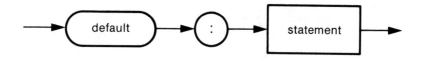

Examples:
```
case 1 : {
        printf ("The value is one \n");
        break;
        }
default: printf ("The value is not one \n");
```

do-while Loop

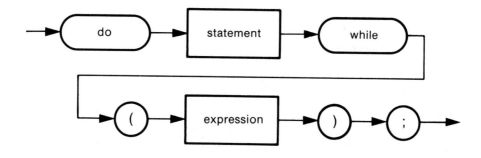

Example:
```
i = 0;
do
 printf ("%d \n", i);
while (i++ <=100);
```

Escape Character

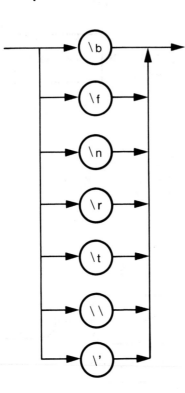

Exponent Value

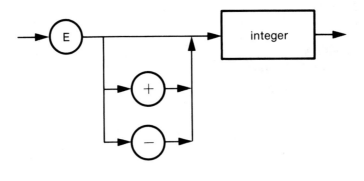

Examples:
E4
E+4
E−4

Expression

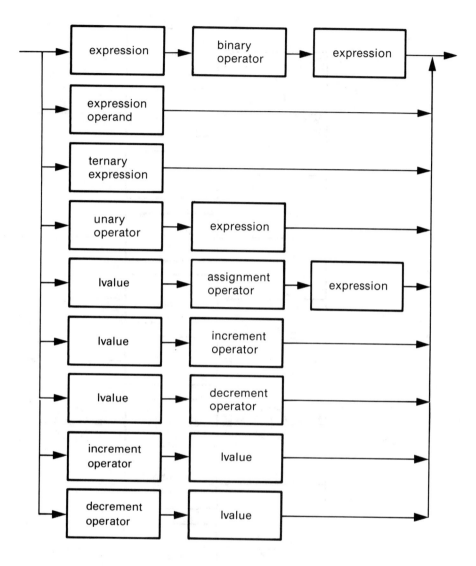

Examples:
```
4
a + b
a
(x> 1) ? 1:0
++ string
* string ++
a = a − 5
```

Expression Operand

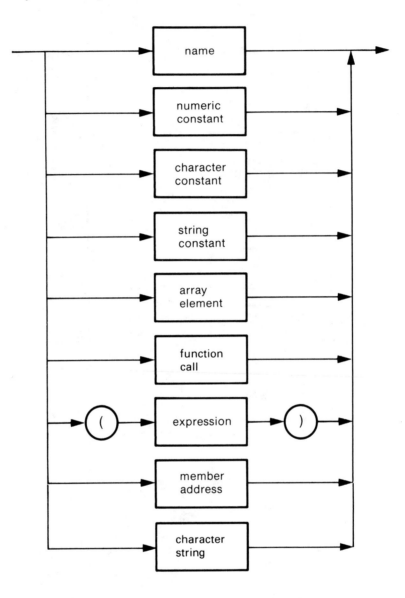

Examples:

```
x + 100      /* name + numeric constant */
a [i] + 'a'  /* array subscript + character constant */
min (x,y)    /* function call */
a + (3 * b)  /* name + (expression) */
             /* (3*b) is a single operand */
```

File Identifier

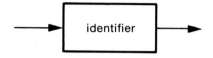

Example:
stdio.h

Floating-Point Constant Value

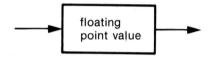

for Loop

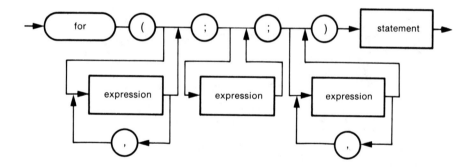

Examples:
```
for (i = 0; i<=10; i++)
  printf ("%d \n", i *i);

for (;;)        /* infinite loop */


for (i = 100, j = 100; j < 109; i++, j++)
  printf ("%d \n", i * j);
```

Floating-Point Value

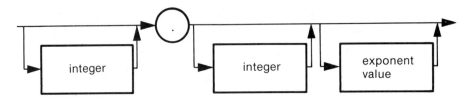

Examples:
```
float y = 123.;
float y = 123.457;
double x = 1.24E-5;
```

Function Body

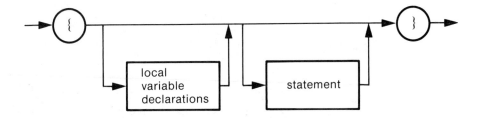

Examples:
```
{
} /* no statements in the function*/

{
 printf ("Error opening output file \n");
}

{
   int count; /* local variable */
   for (count=0; count<=10; count++)
     printf ("%d \n", count);
}
```

Function Call

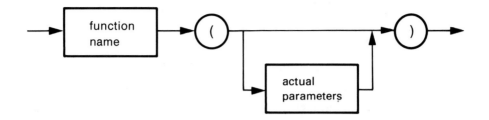

Examples:
clear—screen ( );
printf ("%s", string);
sort (array, num—elements, ascending);

Function Declaration

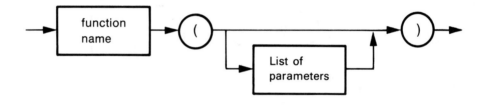

Examples:
clear—screen ( )
min—value (a, b, c)

Function Definition

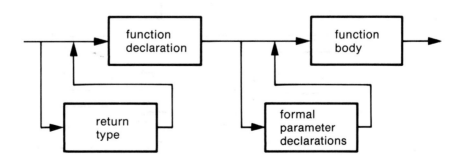

Example:
```
float max__value (a, b)
  float a, b;     /* formal parameters */
{
  return ((a > b) ? a : b);
}
```

Function Name

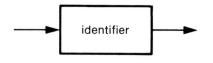

goto Statement

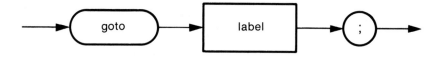

Example:
goto error__message;
error__message: printf ("Invalid data entered \n");

if Statement

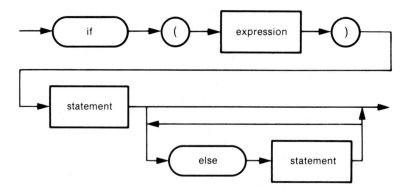

Examples:
```
if (a % 2)
   printf ("%d is odd \n", a);
if (a % 2)
   printf ("%d is odd \n", a);
else
   printf ("%d is even \n", a);
```

Identifier

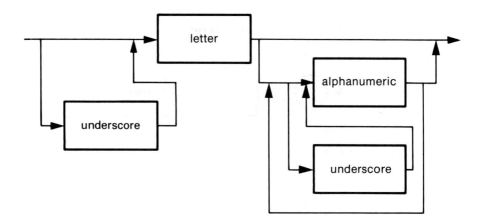

Examples:
```
i
file_name
input_file_name
```

Include Statement

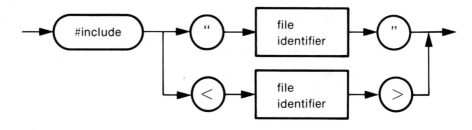

Examples:
```
#include "defn.h"
#include <stdio.h>
```

Increment Operator

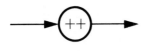

Example:
while (∗string++)
    ;

Indirect Address Reference

Example:
∗string

Initial Value

Integer Constant Value

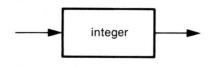

Example:
123

Label

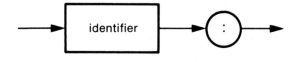

Example:
goto error—message;
error—message: printf(''Invalid data entered \n'');

List of Identifiers

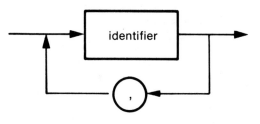

Examples:
a
a, b, c

Local Variable Declarations

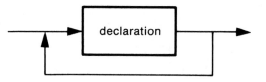

Logical Operator

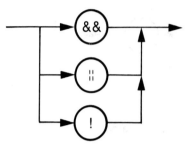

Examples:
```
if (x < 5 && x >0)      /* logical AND */
if (x >= 3 || y<>0)
x = ! 0;                /* assigns x the value 1*/
x = ! 1;                /* assigns x the value 0*/
```

Long Constant

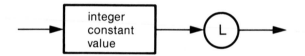

Example:
```
1234567L
```

Macro Declaration

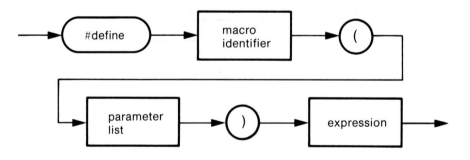

Example:
#define AVERAGE (a,b) ((a+b) / 2)

Macro Identifier

Example:
MAX

Member Address

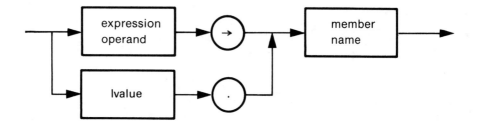

Examples:
student.name
teacher→salary

Member declarations

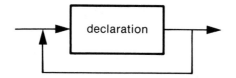

Examples:
int age;
struct students *student;

Member Name

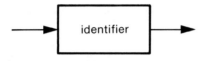

Name

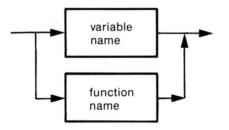

Numeric Constant

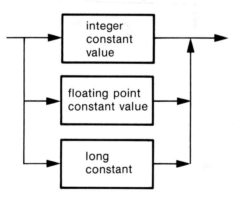

Examples:
123
123.456
123445L

NULL Statement

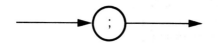

Example:
while (∗string1++=∗string2++)
  ;

Object

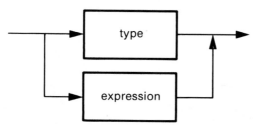

Examples:
struct name — list
array — of — values

Parameter Declarations

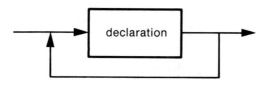

Examples:
int i;
float sum, average;

Pointer Declaration

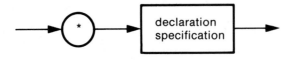

Pointer Expression

Parameter List

Examples:
average
array, num—elements, ascending

Program

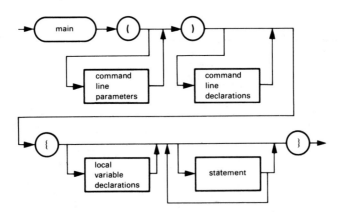

Examples:
```
main( )
  {
     /* no executable statements */
  }

main ( )
  {
     clear__screen ( );
  }

main (argc, argv)
     int argc;        /* command line declarations */
     char *argv[];
  {
     int count;       /* local variable declarations */
     print__file (argv[1]);
  }
```

Relational Operator

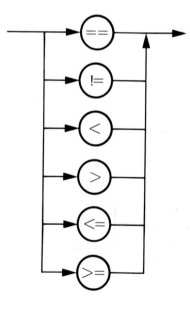

Examples:
```
while (x!=0)
  printf ("%d \n",x--);
if (x<0)
  printf ("x is a negative value \n");
```

Return Statement

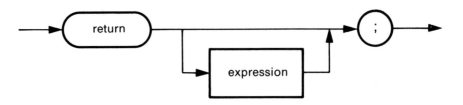

Examples:
```
return;
return (1);
return ((a > b) ? a : b);
```

Return Type

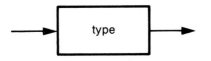

Example:
float

Sizeof Operator

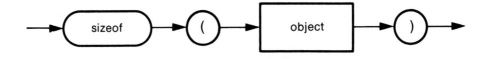

Examples:
```
num_bytes = sizeof (string);
space_required = sizeof (struct address);
word_size = sizeof (int);
```

Statement

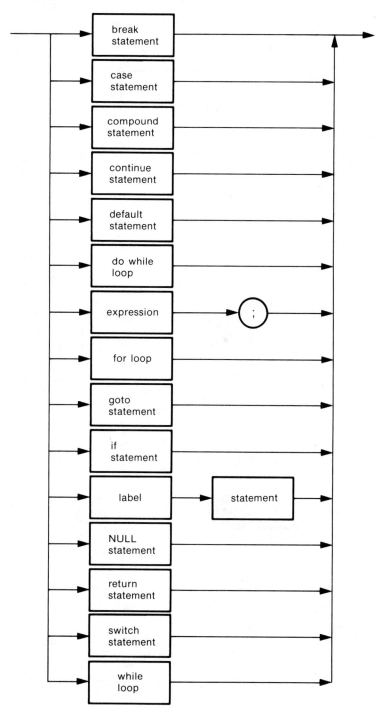

String Constant

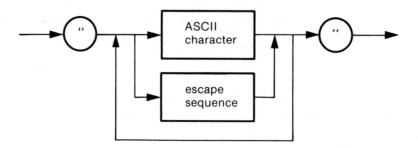

Example:

" \n \n Example String \n \n"

Structure

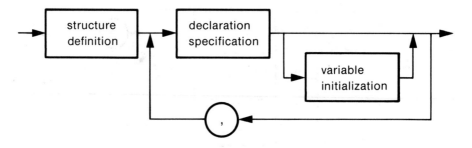

Examples:

struct student class [num—students];

struct address {
  char street[MAX—STREET];
  char city—st—zip [MAX—ADDRESS];
} home—address, work—address;

Structure definition

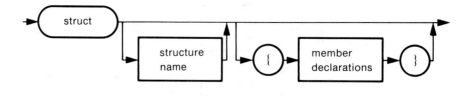

Examples:

```
struct name—list {
  char name [MAX—NAME];
  struct name—list *next;
}

struct student
```

Switch Statement

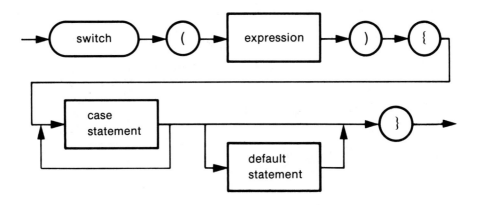

Example:

```
switch (a){
    case 1:  {
                printf ("Only one test score present \n");
                break;
             }
    case 2:  {
                printf ("Two test scores present \n");
                break;
             }
    default: {
                printf (Invalid number of test \n");
                exit (1);
             }
}
```

Type

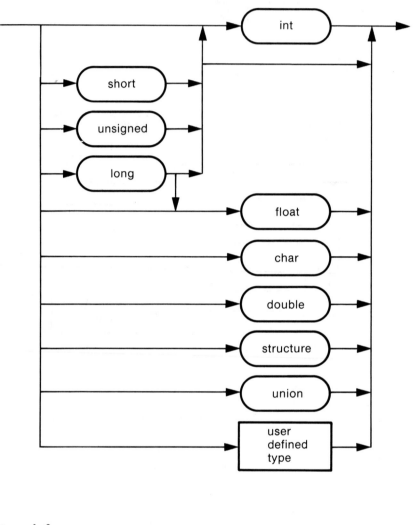

typedef

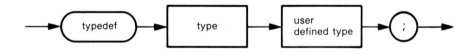

Example:
typedef int counting—numbers;

Ternary Expression

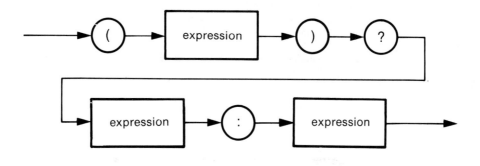

Example:
max = (a > b) ? a :b;

Unary Operator

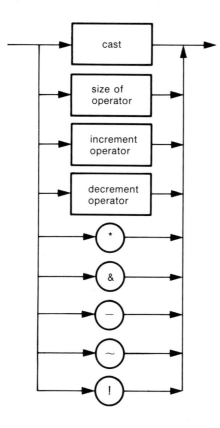

Examples:
```
x = (int) 3.44;
num__bytes = sizeof (string);
address = & variable; /* memory location of variable */
value = *address;
i = −7;
value = *address++; /* assign value and increment address */
```

Union

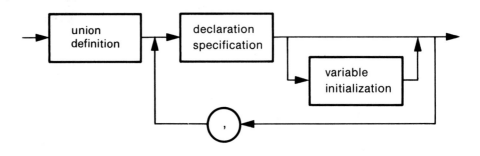

Examples:
```
union zip zip__code;

union zip {
   char long__zip[MAX__ZIP];
   int short__zip;
} zip__code;
```

Union definition

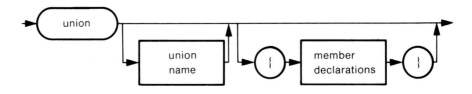

Example:
```
union zip {
   char long__code[9];
   int short__code;
}
```

lvalue

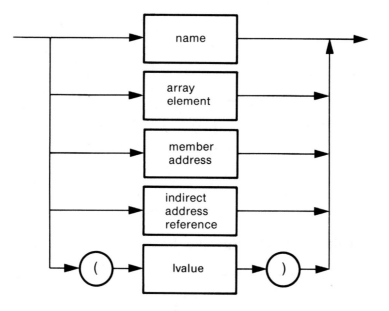

Examples:

big—variable
a[i]
student→score
string / indirect address reference */

Variable Initialization

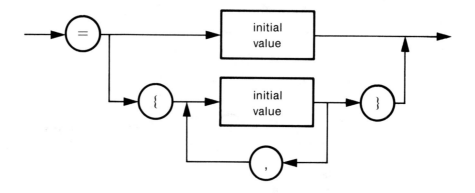

Examples:
x = 37
int a[3] = {0, 1, 2}
int a=3, b=2, c=4

Variable Name

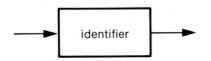

Example:
argc

Variable Storage Specification

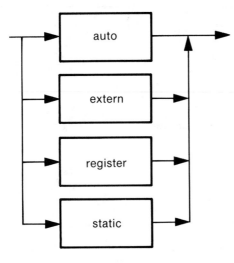

while loop

Example:
    while (i <= 10)
        i++;

C H A P T E R

Constants and Macros

C allows programmers to create constants within programs. The primary advantages of using constants are increased portability, changeability, and readability. In addition, errors in a routine cannot affect the value contained within a constant.

Constants in C are created via the #**define** statement. For example, the following statement creates a constant that is called NUM — CLIENTS and assigns it the value 500.

```
#define NUM_CLIENTS 500
```

The blanks between each word in the constant definition serve as delimiters. Because of this, all expressions will be grouped within parentheses in the macros later in this chapter.

It is good programming style to use uppercase letters for constants and lowercase letters for variable names. Using uppercase letters will increase the readability of your code. In the following **for** loop, for example, another programmer who is reading your code will know that NUM—CLIENTS is a constant because it is in uppercase:

```
for (i = 1; i <= NUM_CLIENTS; i++)
```

Portability is a measure of the ease with which a program that was written and runs on one computer (an IBM PC for example) can be made to run on a different type of computer (an Apple for instance). Constants increase the portability and changeability of routines by limiting the number of changes required. Many of the routines in this text define the end-of-file (EOF) as −1. Some systems, however, represent EOF with a different value. If you define EOF as a constant, the #**define EOF** statement is the only statement you would have to change in your code if you move to a system that represents the end-of-file as 0.

Constants also increase the readability of code by allowing you to assign meaningful names to values and expressions that may not be meaningful to someone who is reading your program. For example, since most systems use the **newline** escape character (\n) as the end of line (EOL) indicator, you can define the constant EOL within your routines to increase readability:

```
for (i = 0; string [i] != EOL && string [i] != EOF; ++i)
                              vs.
for (i = 0; string [i] != '\n' && string [i] != -1; ++i)
```

It is important that you understand how the preprocessor uses the constants you define. For example, if you define the constant **STRING—SIZE** as

```
#define STRING_SIZE 512
```

and then declare the character strings

```
char buffer [STRING_SIZE];
char string [STRING_SIZE];
```

the preprocessor will locate the constant **STRING—SIZE** in the symbol table and substitute the value related to **STRING—SIZE** (512) each time **STRING—SIZE** is referenced within the routine as follows:

```
char buffer [512];
char string [512];
```

The rationale for using blanks as delimiters within constant definitions should now become apparent. If, for example, the constant **STRING—SIZE** was defined as

```
#define STRING_SIZE 512;
```

the substitution would result in an error due to the semicolon:

```
char string [512;];
```

The constants in Table 2-1 are used in many of the routines in this book and they have been placed in a file called **defn.h**.

Most C compilers provide a file called **stdio.h** that contains several definitions required for character I/O and file manipulation. Print this file and examine the definitions provided by your C compiler. To use the definitions provided in **stdio.h**, you must use the **#include** statement.

Once you have created your constants, you can store them in a file so all of your routines can access them and you won't have to type them in for each new program. Chapter 10 will develop a program that reads a file in search of **#include** statements and places the actual constants defined within the source file. This decreases development time since you don't have to type each definition in every program. In addition, your documentation is not affected because the program that substitutes the actual files in place of the **#include** statement produces a very meaningful source file.

Once you have placed all of the constant declarations into a file called **defn.h**, you must include (using **#include**) this file in your program prior to **main()** as follows:

```
#include "defn.h"
```

The quotes around the file name direct the compiler to search the user's default directory file for **defn.h** and then the standard library

Table 2-1.   *Commonly Used Constants*

Constant	Meaning
#define NULL '\0'	/* define the NULL character */
#define EOL '\n'	/* define the end of line */
#define EOF −1	/* define end-of-file */
#define ERROR −1	/* define ERROR return status code */
#define NEWLINE '\n'	/* define carriage return/line feed */
#define BACKSPACE '\b'	
#define CARRIAGE_RETURN '\r'	
#define FORMFEED '\f'	
#define TRUE 1	/* Boolean TRUE in C */
#define FALSE 0	/* Boolean FALSE */
#define PI 3.141592653	
#define MAX_STRING 255	/* max-size strings are dimensioned to */
#define IO_ERROR −1	/* value returned if user enters bad data from the keyboard */
#define NO_ERROR 0	
#define UNDEFINED −9999.9999	/* used in trigonometric functions */
#define BLANK ' '	
#define print_character(x) putch(x)	/* for console I/O */
#define get_character(x) getch(x)	/* for console I/O */

files. If you instead use brackets, for example, **<stdio.h>**, the compiler will only search the standard libraries for the file. The extension **.h** informs the compiler that the file is a *header* file containing constant declarations. As you will see, C also allows you to include files (with **#include**) containing C source code. In this case the file will have the **.c** notation.

Macros

C also allows you to create macros that are expanded in line within programs. The following macro, for example, squares the value contained in the variable **x**:

```
#define square (x) ((x)*(x))
```

Each time the macro is referenced within the program, the compiler will perform a replace. For example, the statement

```
x = square(5);
```

is replaced with

```
x = 5*5;
```

in the executable version of the program. Macros save the overhead of placing variables onto the stack, which is associated with functions. In addition, macros increase the readability of code by replacing expressions with meaningful names.

Most C compilers provide several macros in the file **ctype.h**. Print this file and examine the macros provided by your compiler. Since the C compiler provides several constants that are specific to the system, the preprocessor **#ifndef** can be used. The **#ifndef** preprocessor examines the identifier specified to see if it is defined. If the identifier is not defined, the code between the **#ifndef** and the **#endif** is compiled for later execution. In this case, if the identifier is undefined, it can be defined as follows:

```
#ifndef EOF        /* see if it is undefined */
#define EOF -1     /* if so define it */
#endif
```

Macros and constants are powerful tools. If a value does not change within a program, you should define it as a constant. The routines provided in the remainder of this text make extensive use of constants and macros, thereby providing increased portability, changeability, and readability.

The following macros have been placed in the files **math.h** and **strings.h**, which are required by many of the routines in later chapters.

```
/*
 * NAME: percent(x,y)
 *
 * FUNCTION: Returns the percentage of x / y.
 *
 * EXAMPLES: a = percent(3.0, 4.0);    assigns a the value 75.0
 *
 * VARIABLES USED: x: the dividend.
 *                 y: the divisor.
 *
 * PSEUDO CODE: multiply x by 100.0 (also converts to float)
 *              divide x by y.
 *
 */

#define percent(x, y) (100.0 *  x / y)
```

```
/*
 *   NAME: abs_val(x)
 *
 *   FUNCTION: Returns the absolute value of the value contained
 *             in the variable x.
 *
 *   EXAMPLES:    x = abs_val(-2);     assigns x the value 2
 *               x = abs_val(4);      assigns x the value 4
 *               x = abs_val(4 - 13); assigns x the value 9
 *
 *   VARIABLES USED: x: the expression to return the absolute value of.
 *
 *   PSEUDO CODE:  if (x is positive)
 *                    return (x)
 *                 else
 *                    return (-x)
 *
 */

#define abs_val(x) ((x >= 0) ? x : 0 - x)
```

```
/*
 * NAME: max(x, y)
 *
 * FUNCTION: Returns the maximum value contained in either x or y.
 *
 * EXAMPLES:    x = max(3, 4);       assigns x the value 4
 *              x = max(4, 4);       assigns x the value 4
 *              x = max(4*3, 4+3);   assigns x the value 12
 *
 * VARIABLES USED: x, y: values to compare for maximum.
 *
 * PSEUDO CODE:  if (x is greater than y)
 *                       return (x)
```

```
*              else
*                     return (y)
*
*/

#define max(x, y) ((x > y) ? x : y)
```

```
/*
 * NAME: min(x, y)
 *
 * FUNCTION: Returns the minimum value contained in either x or y.
 *
 * EXAMPLES:    x = min(3, 4);       assigns x the value 3
 *              x = min(3*3, 3+3);   assigns x the value 6
 *
 * VARIABLES USED: x, y: values to compare for minimum.
 *
 * PSEUDO CODE:    if (x is less than y)
 *                      return (x)
 *                 else
 *                      return (y)
 *
 */

#define min(x, y) ((x < y) ? x : y)
```

```
/*
 * NAME: is_odd(x)
 *
 * FUNCTION: Returns 1 if the value contained in x is odd, otherwise
 *           returns the value 0.  The mod operator (%) returns the
 *           remainder of the integer division of x and 2.  If the
 *           remainder is 0, then x is even.  If the remainder is 1
 *           then x is odd.
 *
 * EXAMPLES:    if (is_odd(3))     returns 1
 *              if (is_odd(444))   returns 0
 *
 * VARIABLES USED: x: variable examined to see if it is odd.
 *
 * PSEUDO CODE:    if (x is odd)
 *                      return (1)     -- the Boolean TRUE
 *                 else
 *                      return (0)     -- the Boolean FALSE
 *
 */

#define is_odd(x) ((x % 2 == 1) ? 1 : 0)
```

```
/*
 * NAME: is_even(x)
 *
 * FUNCTION: Returns 1 if the value contained in x is even, otherwise
 *           returns the value 0.  The mod operator (%) returns the
 *           remainder of the integer division of x and 2.  If the
 *           remainder is 0, then x is even.  If the remainder is 1
 *           then x is odd.
 *
 * EXAMPLES:    if (is_even(30))      returns 1
 *              if (is_even(4445))    returns 0
 *
 * VARIABLES USED: x: variable examined to see if it is even.
 *
 * PSEUDO CODE:  if (x is even)
 *                  return (1)       -- the Boolean TRUE
 *               else
 *                  return (0)       -- the Boolean FALSE
 *
 */

#define is_even(x) ((x % 2 == 0) ? 1 : 0)
```

```
/*
 * NAME: round_off(x)
 *
 * FUNCTION: Rounds off the value contained in x.
 *
 * EXAMPLES:    i = round_off(3.443);       assigns i the value 3
 *              i = round_off(3.55);        assigns i the value 4
 *
 * VARIABLES USED:  x: contains the value to round off.
 *
 * PSEUDO CODE:  add 0.5 to the value for rounding
 *               cast the value to the type int
 *
 */

#define round_off(x) ((int)(x + 0.5))
```

```
/*
 * NAME: truncate(x)
 *
 * FUNCTION: Truncates the value contained in x.
 *
 * EXAMPLES:    i = truncate(3.443);        assigns i the value 3
 *              i = truncate(0.11 - 0.05);  assigns i the value 0
 *
 * VARIABLES USED:  x: contains the value to truncate.
 *
 * PSEUDO CODE:  cast the value to the type int
 *
```

```
*/

#define truncate(x) ((int)(x))
```

```
/*
 * NAME:  remainder(x, y)
 *
 * FUNCTION:   Uses the mod (%) operator to return the remainder
 *             of the integer division of the values in x and y.
 *
 * EXAMPLES:    i = remainder(10, 3);  assigns i the value 1  (3 R 1)
 *              i = remainder(3, 3);   assigns i the value 0  (1 R 0)
 *
 * VARIABLES USED: x: the dividend.
 *                 y: the divisor.
 *
 * PSEUDO CODE:  mod the value contained in x by the value contained
 *               in y to produce the remainder
 *
 */

#define remainder(x, y) (x % y)
```

```
/*
 * NAME: square(x)
 *
 * FUNCTION: Returns the square of the value contained in x.
 *
 * EXAMPLE: y = square(9);    assigns y the value 81
 *
 * VARIABLES USED: x: contains the value to be squared.
 *
 * PSEUDO CODE: multiply the value contained in x times itself
 *
 */

#define square (x) ((x)*(x))
```

```
/*
 * NAME: cube(x)
 *
 * FUNCTION: Returns the cube of the value contained in x.
 *
 * EXAMPLE: y = cube(9); assigns y the value 729 (9 * 9 * 9)
 *
 * VARIABLES USED: x: contains the value to be cubed.
 *
```

```
 *  PSEUDO CODE: multiply the value contained in x times itself twice
 *               (cube(4) ==> 4 * 4 * 4)
 */

#define cube (x) ((x)*(x)*(x))
```

```
/*
 * NAME: XOR(x,y)
 *
 * FUNCTION: Returns the exclusive or of the bits contained in
 *           the variables x and y.
 *
 *           The exclusive or uses the following truth table:
 *
 *               x    y     result
 *               0    0       0
 *               0    1       1
 *               1    0       1
 *               1    1       0   <--- note
 *
 * VARIABLES USED: x, y: contain the values to be exclusive or'd.
 *
 * PSEUDO CODE: invert (via ones complement) the value in y
 *              bitwise AND x and the value of y inverted
 *
 *              invert the value contained in x
 *              bitwise AND the value in y with value of x inverted
 *
 *              perform a bitwise OR of the result of the expressions
 *              above
 *
 */

#define XOR(x, y) ((x & ~y) | (~x & y))
```

```
/*
 * NAME: NOT(x)
 *
 * FUNCTION: Returns the Boolean NOT of the value contained in x.
 *           If x is TRUE, FALSE is returned.  If x is FALSE, TRUE
 *           is returned.
 *
 * EXAMPLE: while (NOT(done))
 *
 * VARIABLES USED: x: contains the value to NOT.
 *
 * PSEUDO CODE: if (x is > 0) (Boolean false)
 *                  return (0)                 -- Boolean FALSE
 *              else
 *                  return (1)                 -- Boolean TRUE
 *
 */

#define NOT(x) ((x != 0) ? 0 : 1)
```

```
/*
 * NAME bit_mask(x, y)
 *
 * FUNCTION: Performs a bitwise AND on the contents of x and y.
 *
 * EXAMPLE: mask = bit_mask(1, 3); assigns mask the value 1
 *
 *             0001 & 0011 produces 0001
 *
 * VARIABLES USED: x, y: contain values to mask.
 *
 * PSEUDO CODE: perform a bitwise AND (&) on each bit in the
 *              values contained in x and y.
 *
 */

#define bit_mask(x, y) (x & y)
```

```
/*
 * NAME: is_digit(x)
 *
 * FUNCTION: Returns 1 if x is a character in the range '0' to '9'
 *           otherwise returns 0.
 *
 * EXAMPLES:      if (is_digit('7'))      returns 1
 *                if (is_digit('a'))      returns 0
 *
 * VARIABLES USED: x: variable examined to see if it is a digit.
 *
 * PSEUDO CODE:  if (x is in the range '0' to '9')
 *                   return (1)    -- the Boolean TRUE
 *               else
 *                   return (0)    -- the Boolean FALSE
 *
 */

#define is_digit(x) ((x >= '0' && x <= '9') ? 1 : 0)
```

```
/*
 * NAME: is_uppercase(x)
 *
 * FUNCTION: Returns 1 if x is an UPPERCASE letter, otherwise returns
 *           the value 0.
 *
 * EXAMPLES:      if (is_uppercase('S'))      returns 1
 *                if (is_uppercase('9'))      returns 0
 *                if (is_uppercase('a'))      returns 0
 *
 * VARIABLES USED: x: variable examined for UPPERCASE.
 *
```

```
*  PSEUDO CODE:   if (x is in the range 'A' to 'Z')
*                    return (1)    -- the Boolean TRUE
*                 else
*                    return (0)    -- the Boolean FALSE
*
*/

#define is_uppercase(x) ((x >= 'A' && x <= 'Z') ? 1 : 0)
```

```
/*
* NAME: is_lowercase(x)
*
* FUNCTION: Returns 1 if x is a lowercase letter, otherwise returns
*           the value 0.
*
* EXAMPLES:    if (is_lowercase('s'))      returns 1
*              if (is_lowercase('9'))      returns 0
*              if (is_lowercase('A'))      returns 0
*
* VARIABLES USED: x: variable examined for lowercase.
*
* PSEUDO CODE:   if (x is in the range 'a' to 'z')
*                    return (1)    -- the Boolean TRUE
*                 else
*                    return (0)    -- the Boolean FALSE
*
*/

#define is_lowercase(x) ((x >= 'a' &&  x <= 'z') ? 1 : 0)
```

```
/*
* NAME: is_blank(x)
*
* FUNCTION: Returns 1 if the value contained in x is a blank,
*           otherwise returns 0.
*
* EXAMPLES:    if (is_blank(' '))      returns 1
*              if (is_blank('a'))      returns 0
*
*              while (is_blank(string[index++]))   -- skips blanks
*
* VARIABLES USED: x: variable to examine for a blank.
*
* PSEUDO CODE:   if (x is a blank)
*                    return (1) -- the Boolean TRUE
*                 else
*                    return (0) -- the Boolean FALSE
*
*/

#define is_blank(x) ((x == ' ') ? 1 : 0)
```

```
/*
 * NAME: BELL
 *
 * FUNCTION:   Rings the computer bell.
 *
 * EXAMPLES:   for (i = 1; i < 10; i++)
 *                   BELL;
 *
 * VARIABLES USED: None.
 *
 * PSEUDO CODE: Use putchar() to output an ASCII 7 for the Bell
 *
 */

#define BELL putchar(7)
```

```
/*
 * NAME: to_uppercase(x)
 *
 * FUNCTION: Converts the character contained in the variable x
 *           to UPPERCASE if it is a lowercase letter, otherwise
 *           it is unchanged.
 *
 * EXAMPLES: to_uppercase('4');  returns '4'
 *           to_uppercase('a');  returns 'A'
 *
 * VARIABLES USED: x: contains the letter to convert to
 *                    UPPERCASE.
 *
 * PSEUDO CODE:  if (x is lowercase)
 *                   convert it to uppercase
 *               else
 *                   return the letter
 *
 */

#define to_uppercase(x) ((is_lowercase(x)) ? x - 'a' + 'A' : x)
```

```
/*
 * NAME: to_lowercase(x)
 *
 * FUNCTION: Converts the character contained in the variable x
 *           to lowercase if it is a UPPERCASE letter, otherwise
 *           it is unchanged.
 *
 * EXAMPLES: to_lowercase('4');  returns '4'
 *           to_lowercase('A');  returns 'a'
 *
 * VARIABLES USED: x: contains the letter to convert to
 *                    lowercase.
 *
```

```
* PSEUDO CODE:  if (x is UPPERCASE)
*                     convert it to lowercase
*               else
*                     return the letter
*
*/

#define to_lowercase(x) ((is_uppercase(x)) ? x + 'a' - 'A' : x)
```

```
/*
 * NAME: to_decimal(x)
 *
 * FUNCTION: Converts the ASCII digit to the corresponding decimal
 *           value.  Assumes x has been verified as a digit by the
 *           macro is_digit().
 *
 * EXAMPLE: x = to_decimal('3'); assigns x the value 3
 *
 * VARIABLES USED: x: character to convert to decimal.
 *
 * PSEUDO CODE: convert x to decimal by subtracting '0'
 *
 *              '3' - '0' = 51 - 48 (Decimal) = 3
 *
 */

#define to_decimal(x) (x - '0')
```

```
/*
 * NAME: is_control(x)
 *
 * FUNCTION: Returns 1 if the value contained in x is a control
 *           character, otherwise 0 is returned.
 *
 * EXAMPLE: is_control('a')  returns 0
 *          is_control(14)   returns 1
 *
 * VARIABLES USED: x: letter to examine.
 *
 * PSEUDO CODE: if (x is > 0 and x is < 32) -- ASCII control characters
 *                     return (1)                -- Boolean TRUE
 *               else
 *                     return (0)                -- Boolean FALSE
 *
 */

#define is_control(x) ((x > 0 && x < 32) ? 1 : 0)
```

```
/*
 * NAME: is_printable_ascii(x)
 *
 * FUNCTION: Returns 1 if x is a printable ASCII character, or
 *           0 if x is not printable.
 *
 * EXAMPLE: if (is_printable_ascii(44))
 *
 * VARIABLES USED: x: contains the ASCII character to examine.
 *
 * PSEUDO CODE: if (x is > 32 and x is < 127)
 *                   return (1)   -- Boolean TRUE
 *              else
 *                   return (0)   -- Boolean FALSE
 *
 */

#define is_printable_ascii(x) ((x > 32 && x < 127) ? 1 : 0)
```

```
/*
 * NAME: to_ascii(x)
 *
 * FUNCTION: Converts an integer in the range 0 - 9 to its
 *           ASCII character representation.  The value -1
 *           is returned if the value is not in the range
 *           0 - 9.
 *
 * EXAMPLE: letter = to_ascii(7); assigns letter the value 55
 *
 * VARIABLES USED: x: contains the integer value to convert.
 *
 * PSEUDO CODE: if (x is >= 0 and x is <= 9)
 *                   return (the ASCII representation by adding '0')
 *              else
 *                   return (-1)
 *
 */

#define to_ascii(x) ((x >= 0 && x <= 9) ? x + '0' : -1)
```

```
/*
 * NAME: is_binary(x)
 *
 * FUNCTION: Returns TRUE if x contains a '1' or '0', otherwise
 *           FALSE is returned.
 *
 * EXAMPLE: if (is_binary('4'))     returns 0
 *
 * VARIABLES USED: x: contains the ASCII character to examine.
 *
```

```
 *  PSEUDO CODE: if (x equals '0' or x equals '1')
 *                  return (1)  -- Boolean TRUE
 *              else
 *                  return (0)  -- Boolean FALSE
 *
 */

#define is_binary(x) ((x == '0' || x == '1') ? 1 : 0)
```

```
/*
 *  NAME: is_hexadecimal(x)
 *
 *  FUNCTION: Returns 1 if the value contained in x is hexadecimal
 *            (e.g. in the range 0 - 9 or A - F), otherwise the value
 *            0 is returned.
 *
 *  EXAMPLE: while (is_hexadecimal(x))
 *
 *  VARIABLES USED: x: contains the ASCII character to examine.
 *
 *  PSEUDO CODE: if (x is a digit or (x >= 'A' and x <= 'F'))
 *                  return (1)  -- Boolean TRUE
 *              else
 *                  return (0)  -- Boolean FALSE
 *
 */

#define is_hexadecimal(x) ((is_digit(x) || (x >= 'A' && x <= 'F'))? 1:0)
```

```
/*
 *  NAME: is_octal(x)
 *
 *  FUNCTION: Returns 1 if the value contained in x is octal
 *            (in the range '0' - '7'), otherwise the value
 *            0 is returned.
 *
 *  EXAMPLE: while (is_octal(x))
 *
 *  VARIABLES USED: x: contains the ASCII character to examine.
 *
 *  PSEUDO CODE: if (x is >= '0' and x is <= '7')
 *                  return (1)     -- Boolean TRUE
 *              else
 *                  return (0)     -- Boolean FALSE
 *
 */

#define is_octal(x) ((x >= '0' && x <= '7') ? 1 : 0)
```

C H A P T E R

3

String Manipulation

String manipulation is often a large part of any programming task, but by creating a library of string manipulation routines, you can greatly decrease the development time of many applications. C is one of the few programming languages that provide the programmer with the internal representation of character strings. As you will see, this access allows you to create several powerful programming tools. Before examining the string manipulation routines in this chapter, let's first review the internal representation of character strings in C.

Character strings in C are stored as arrays; that is, successive characters are stored in contiguous memory locations. To create a string variable, you must allocate enough space for the number of characters in the string and the NULL character (\0) that is appended to all string variables and constants. For example, if you want to create a string variable capable of storing the word "Computer," you can declare the string as follows:

```
char string[9];
```

When the string is assigned the word "Computer," the characters are stored in memory as follows:

C
o
m
p
u
t
e
r
\0

The C compiler will append the NULL character to all character constants for you. For example, if you define the constant vowels,

```
#define VOWELS "aeiouAEIOU"
```

the constant is stored in memory as

a
e
i
o
u
A
E
I
O
U
\0

When creating character strings, however, you must append the NULL character to the end of the string. Since the NULL character is appended to all of the strings, searching for the end of the string can be done as follows:

```
for (index = 0; string[index] != NULL; index++)
```

As you will see, the majority of the routines in this chapter search for the end of the string in this manner. In Chapter 4 you will see how many of these routines can be implemented with pointers instead of character arrays. In this chapter, though, several of the routines assume that the strings are capable of containing MAX_STRING characters. MAX_STRING is defined to be 255 in Chapter 2.

The importance of string manipulation routines will become more readily apparent when these routines are used to implement the complex programs in later chapters. Each of the file manipulation routines in Chapter 10 utilizes the string manipulation tools.

The development of these rather complex routines was greatly sim-
plified by using the string manipulation routines in this chapter.

```
/*
 * NAME: string_length (string)
 *
 * FUNCTION: Returns a count of the number of characters
 *           in the variable string.  The string is examined
 *           character by character until NULL is found.
 *
 * EXAMPLE: length = string_length ("this string");
 *              assigns length the value 11
 *
 * VARIABLES USED: string: contains the string to be examined.
 *                 count: index into the character string.
 *
 * PSEUDO CODE:  initialize count to 0
 *
 *               while (the character in string[count] is not NULL)
 *                   increment count -- which contains the number of
 *                                      characters in the string
 *               return (count)
 *
 */
string_length (string)
  char string[];          /* string to examine */
  {
  int count;              /* number of characters in the string */

  for (count = 0; string [count] != NULL; ++count)
     ;

  return (count);         /* number of characters in the string */
  }
```

```
/*
 * NAME: copy_string (string1, string2)
 *
 * FUNCTION: Copies the contents of string1 to string2.
 *
 * EXAMPLE:  copy_string ("string to copy", my_string);
 *
 *           copies the string "string to copy" to the character
 *           string my_string.
 *
```

```
* VARIABLES USED: string1: string to copy.
*                 string2: string receiving copy.
*                 index: index into the character strings.
*
* PSEUDO CODE:  initialize index to 0
*
*               while (string2[index] is assigned the value in
*                   string1[index] and string1[index] is not NULL)
*                   increment index to point to the next letter
*
* NOTE: When (string2[index] = string1[index]) is equal to NULL,
*       string2[index] will have been assigned the NULL value as
*       desired and the loop will terminate.
*
*/

copy_string (string1, string2)
  char string1[];              /* string to be copied */
  char string2[];
 {
  int index;

  /* by placing parentheses around

            string2[index] = string1[index]

  the value contained in string1[index] is first assigned
  to string2[index] and then the Boolean test is
  performed on the value that was assigned.  As long as
  string2[index] is not assigned NULL the loop will continue */

  for (index = 0; (string2[index] = string1[index]) != NULL; index++)
      ;
 }
```

```
/*
 * NAME: append_string (string1, string2)
 *
 * FUNCTION: Appends the contents of string1 to the contents
 *           of string2.
 *
 * EXAMPLE:  string1      string2 before    string2 after
 *           " there!"       "Hello"        "Hello there!"
 *
 *           append_string (string1, string2);
 *
 * VARIABLES USED:  string1: string to append.
 *                  string2: string being appended to.
 *                  index1:  index into string1.
 *                  index2:  index into string2.
 *
```

```
* PSEUDO CODE:   initialize index2 to 0
*
*               while (string2[index2] is not NULL)
*                   increment index2  -- to find the end of string2
*
*               initialize index1 to 0
*
*               while (string2[index2] is assigned the letter in
*                       string1[index1] and the letter is not NULL)
*                   increment index1 and index2
*
*/
append_string (string1, string2)
   char string1[];                  /* string to append */
   char string2[];                  /* string appended to */
 {
   int index1;     /* current location in string1 */
   int index2;     /* current location in string2 */

   /* find the end of string2 */

   for (index2 = 0; string2[index2] != NULL; index2++)
     ;

   /* append string1 to string2 */

   for (index1 = 0;(string2[index2] = string1[index1])!= NULL; ++index1)
       ++index2;   /* also increment string2 */
 }
```

```
/*
 * NAME: string_swap (string1, string2)
 *
 * FUNCTION: Exchanges the characters contained in string1 with the
 *           the characters contained in string2.
 *
 * EXAMPLE: string1      string2  before      string1      string2  after
 *          "Hello"        "There"            "There"        "Hello"
 *
 *          string_swap (string1, string2);
 *
 * VARIABLES USED: string1, string2: contain the strings to swap.
 *                 temp: temporary storage for string1.
 *
 * ROUTINES CALLED: copy_string()  copies the first string specified
 *                                 to the second string.
 *
 * PSEUDO CODE:  copy the contents of string1 to the temporary
 *               string temp
 *
```

```
*                   copy the contents of string2 to string1
*
*                   copy the contents of the temporary string
*                   to string2
*
*/

string_swap (string1, string2)
  char string1[];
  char string2[];
 {
  char temp[MAX_STRING];     /* maximum string size */

  /* save the contents of string1 */

  copy_string (string1, temp);

  /* swap string2 */

  copy_string (string2, string1);

  /* place the previous contents of string1 into string2 */

  copy_string (temp, string2);
 }
```

```
/*
 * NAME: str_to_uppercase (string)
 *
 * FUNCTION: Converts the contents of a string to UPPERCASE.
 *
 * EXAMPLES: if string contains "this is it!"
 *           str_to_uppercase (string); => THIS IS IT!
 *
 *           if string contains "tHIS is It!"
 *           str_to_uppercase (string); => THIS IS IT!
 *
 * VARIABLES USED: string: string to convert to UPPERCASE.
 *                 index: index into the character string.
 *
 * MACROS USED: to_uppercase();  converts a character to UPPERCASE.
 *
 * PSEUDO CODE:   initialize index to 0
 *
 *                while (string[index] is not NULL)
 *                  convert string[index] to UPPERCASE
 *                  increment index to point to the next letter
 *
 */
```

```
str_to_uppercase (string)
  char string[];
 {
  int index;  /* index into the string */

  /* convert each letter in the string to UPPERCASE */

  for (index = 0; string[index] != NULL; ++index)
     string[index] = to_uppercase(string[index]);
 }
```

```
/*
 * NAME: str_to_lowercase (string)
 *
 * FUNCTION: Converts the contents of a string to lowercase.
 *
 * EXAMPLES: if string contains  "THIS IS IT!"
 *           str_to_lowercase (string); => this is it!
 *
 *           if string contains "tHIS is It!"
 *           str_to_lowercase (string); => this is it!
 *
 * VARIABLES USED: string: string to convert to lowercase.
 *                 index: index into the character string.
 *
 * MACROS USED: to_lowercase();  converts a character to lowercase.
 *
 * PSEUDO CODE:  initialize index to 0
 *
 *                while (string[index] is not NULL)
 *                    convert string[index] to lowercase
 *                    increment index to point to the next letter
 *
 */

str_to_lowercase (string)
  char string[];
 {
  int index;  /* index into the string */

  /* convert each letter in the string to lowercase */

  for (index = 0; string[index] != NULL; ++index)
    string[index] = to_lowercase(string[index]);
 }
```

```
/*
 * NAME: invert_string (string)
 *
 * FUNCTION: Converts lowercase letters in the string to UPPERCASE,
 *           and the UPPERCASE letters to lowercase.
 *
 * EXAMPLES: if string contains "this IS iT!"
 *           invert_string (string);  => THIS is It!"
 *           if string contains "893kk#$#"
 *           invert_string (string);  => 893KK#$#
 *
 * VARIABLES USED: string: string containing the characters to invert.
 *                 index: index into the character string.
 *
 * MACROS USED: to_uppercase();  converts a character to UPPERCASE.
 *              to_lowercase();  converts a character to lowercase.
 *              is_uppercase();  returns 1 if the letter is UPPERCASE
 *                               else 0.
 *              is_lowercase();  returns 1 if the letter is lowercase
 *                               else 0.
 *
 * PSEUDO CODE:  initialize index to 0
 *
 *               while (string[index] is not NULL)
 *                 if (string[index] is UPPERCASE)
 *                   convert it to lowercase
 *                 else if (string[index] is lowercase)
 *                   convert it to UPPERCASE
 *                 else
 *                   don't change it -- number or punctuation
 *
 *               increment index to point to the next letter
 */

invert_string(string)
  char string[];
  {
  int index;    /* index into the character string */

  for (index = 0; string[index] != NULL; ++index)

    if (is_uppercase(string[index]))
      string[index] = to_lowercase(string[index]);

    else if (is_lowercase(string[index]))
      string[index] = to_uppercase(string[index]);
  }
```

```
/*
 * NAME: insert_string (string, substring, location)
 *
 * FUNCTION: Inserts the contents of the substring into the
 *           string at the character location specified.
 *
 * EXAMPLES: string1 = "THIS IT" string2 = "IS "
 *           insert_string (string1, string2, 5); => THIS IS IT
 *           insert_string (string1, string2, 23); => -1 is returned
 *                                                     error in location
 *
 * VARIABLES USED: string: string the substring is inserted into.
 *                 substring: contains the substring to insert.
 *                 temp: temporary string storage.
 *                 index1: index into the string.
 *                 index2: index into the substring.
 *                 index_temp: index into the temporary string.
 *
 * PSEUDO CODE:  if (the insertion location is >= the string length)
 *                   return(-1);  -- error in the starting location
 *
 *               copy the characters in the string prior to the starting
 *               location to the temporary character string temp
 *
 *               append the contents of the substring to the current
 *               contents of the temporary string
 *
 *               append the remainder of the string to the temporary
 *               string
 *
 *               copy the contents of the temporary string back
 *               to the string
 *
 */

insert_string (string, substring, location)
  char string[];
  char substring[];      /* substring to insert */
  int location;          /* character location in the string to
                            insert the substring at */
 {
  int index1;            /* index into the string */
  int index2;            /* index into the substring */
  int index_temp;        /* index into the temporary string */

  char temp[MAX_STRING];

  /* see if the location is valid */

  if (location >= string_length (string))
     return (-1);

  /* copy the characters in the string prior to the
     starting location to the temporary string temp */

  for (index_temp = 0, index1 = 0; index1 < location; index1++,
                                                       index_temp++)

      temp[index_temp] = string[index1];
```

```
/* append the substring to current contents of the temporary string */

for (index2 = 0; substring[index2] != NULL; ++index2, index_temp++)
    temp[index_temp] = substring[index2];

/* append the remainder of the string to the temporary string */

while (temp[index_temp++] = string[index1++])
  ;

/* put contents of the temporary string back into the string */

copy_string (temp, string);
}
```

```
/*
 * NAME: pad_string (string, num_blanks);
 *
 * FUNCTION:   Appends the contents of the variable string to the
 *             number of blanks specified.
 *
 * EXAMPLE:    pad_string (my_string, 5); inserts 5 blanks prior
 *                                        to the first character
 *                                        in my_string.
 *
 * VARIABLES USED:   string: string to place the blanks into.
 *                   num_blanks: number of blanks to insert.
 *                   temp: temporary character string.
 *                   index: index into the string.
 *                   count: count of the number of blanks.
 *
 * ROUTINES CALLED:  append_string();  appends the first string
 *                                     specified to the second.
 *                   copy_string(); copies the first string specified
 *                                  to the second.
 *
 * PSEUDO CODE:  place the number of blanks specified into the
 *               temporary string temp
 *
 *               append the contents of the string to the
 *               temporary string
 *
 *               copy the contents of the temporary string back
 *               to string
 *
 */

pad_string (string, num_blanks)
  char string[];
  int num_blanks;  /* number of blanks */
 {
  int index;
  int count;       /* number of blanks assigned */
```

```
char temp[MAX_STRING];

/* place the blanks into the temporary string */

for (count = 0; count < num_blanks; count++)
    temp[count] = BLANK;

temp[count] = NULL;

/* append the contents of the string to the temporary string */

append_string (string, temp);

/* place the contents of the temporary string back into string */

copy_string (temp, string);
}
```

```
/*
 * NAME: remove_substring (string, first, num_char)
 *
 * FUNCTION: Removes the number of characters specified starting
 *           at the character location contained in first from
 *           the contents of string.
 *
 * EXAMPLES: if string contains "THIS IS IT"
 *
 *           remove_substring (string, 0, 1);  ==> "HIS IS IT"
 *           remove_substring (string, 25, 1); ==> -1 returned error
 *                                                 in location
 *           remove_substring (string, 8, 8);  ==> "THIS IS "
 *
 * VARIABLES USED:  string: string containing the characters to delete.
 *                  first: location of first the character to delete.
 *                  num_char: number of characters to delete.
 *                  index1, index2: indices into the character string.
 *                  length: length of the string.
 *
 * ROUTINES CALLED: string_length(); returns the length of a string.
 *
 * PSEUDO CODE:  get the length of the string
 *
 *               if (the starting location is >= the length of string
 *                   OR the starting location is < 0)
 *                       return (-1) -- invalid starting location
 *
 *               if (the # of letters to delete >= the string length)
 *                       modify the # of characters so that only the
 *                       characters up to NULL are deleted
 *
 *               append the characters remaining in the string
 *               after the deletion to string[first]
 *
 */
```

```
remove_substring (string, first, num_char)
  char string[];
  int first;      /* location of the first character to remove */
  int num_char;   /* number of characters to remove */
{
  int length;     /* length of the string */

  int index1;     /* points to the first character to remove */
  int index2;     /* points to the first character remaining after
                     removal of the other characters */

  length = string_length (string);

  if (first >= length || first < 0)
    return (-1);       /* invalid starting location */

  if (first + num_char <= length)
    index2 = first + num_char;
  else
    index2 = length;  /* only delete to NULL */

  /* remove the characters */

  for (index1 = first; string[index1] = string[index2]; index1++)
    index2++;
}
```

```
/*
 * NAME: right_index (string, character)
 *
 * FUNCTION: Returns the right most location of the letter contained
 *           in character within the string, or -1 if the character was
 *           not found.
 *
 * EXAMPLES:   right_index ("THIS IS IT", 'I');  returns 8
 *             right_index ("THIS IS IT", '0');  returns -1
 *
 * VARIABLES USED: string: string to search for the character.
 *                 character: character we are searching for.
 *                 index: index into the character string.
 *                 right_loc: right most location of the character.
 *
 * PSEUDO CODE:  assign right_loc -1 -- in case the letter is not found
 *               initialize index to 0
 *
 *               while (string[index] is not NULL)
 *                 if (string[index] is equal to the character)
 *                   assign right_loc the value of index
 *                 increment index to point to the next letter
 *
 *               return (right_loc) -- right most location of the
 *                                     character or, -1 if the letter
```

```
 *                                          was not found
 */

right_index (string, character)
  char string[];
  char character;         /* the letter we are searching for */
{
  int right_loc = -1;   /* right most location of the character
                              in the string */
                          /* -1 in case the character is not found */
  int index;

  /* search the string for the character */

  for (index = 0; string [index] != NULL; ++index)
    if (string[index] == character)
      right_loc = index;            /* right most location */
                                    /* continue search for the
                                        next occurrence of the letter */

  return (right_loc);               /* -1 if the character was not found */
}
```

```
/*
 * NAME: str_index (string, substring)
 *
 * FUNCTION: Returns the starting location of the substring
 *           in the string, or the value -1 is the substring was
 *           not found.
 *
 * EXAMPLES: str_index ("This is it", "it"); returns 8
 *           str_index ("This is it", "IT"); returns -1
 *
 * VARIABLES USED:  string: contains the string to search for
 *                          the substring.
 *                  substring: substring we are searching for.
 *                  i, j, k: indices into the character strings.
 *
 * PSEUDO CODE: initialize i to 0
 *
 *              while (string[i] is not NULL)
 *                assign j the value in i and begin looking
 *                for the substring at that point
 *
 *              assign  k the value 0
 *
 *              while (string[j] equals substring[k])
 *                if (substring[k + 1] == NULL)
 *                  return (i) -- the substring exist
 *                else
 *                  increment j, and k
 *
```

```
 *             if (the substring did not exist)
 *                return (-1)
 *
 */

str_index (string, substring)
  char string[];
  char substring[];
{
  int i, j, k;

  for (i = 0; string[i] != NULL; i++)
    for (j = i, k = 0; substring[k] == string[j]; k++, j++)
      if (substring[k+1] == NULL)
          return (i);                    /* the substring was found */

  return (-1);                           /* the substring was not found */
}
```

```
/*
 * NAME: str_count (string, substring)
 *
 * FUNCTION: Returns a count of the number of times the
 *           substring appears in the string.
 *
 * EXAMPLES: str_count ("THIS IS IT", "IS"); returns 2
 *           str_count ("THIS IS IT", "NO"); returns 0
 *
 * VARIABLES USED: string: string to search for the substring.
 *                 substring: substring we are searching for.
 *                 count: number of times the substring occurs
 *                        in the string.
 *                 i, j, k: indices into the character strings.
 *
 * PSEUDO CODE:   initialize index and count to 0
 *
 *                while (string[i] is not NULL)
 *                assign j the value in i and begin looking
 *                for the substring at that point
 *
 *                assign k the value 0
 *
 *                while (string[j] equals substring[k])
 *                   if (substring[k + 1] == NULL)
 *                      increment count -- the substring exist
 *                      break iteration
 *                   else
 *                      increment j, and k
 *
 *                return (count)
 *
 */
```

```
str_count (string, substring)
  char string[];
  char substring[];    /* the substring we are looking for */
{
  int i, j, k;
  int count = 0;        /* count of the occurrences of the substring */

  for (i = 0; string[i] != NULL; i++)
    for (j = i, k = 0; substring[k] == string[j]; k++, j++)
      if (substring[k+1] == NULL)
        {
          count++;       /* the substring was found - increment count */
          break;         /* start looking for the next occurrence */
        }

  return (count);
}
```

```
/*
 * NAME: str_right_index (string, substring)
 *
 * FUNCTION: Returns the right most starting location of the
 *           substring within the string, or -1 if the substring
 *           was not contained in the string.
 *
 * EXAMPLES: str_right_index ("THIS IS IT", "IS"); returns 5
 *           str_right_index ("THIS IS IT", "NO"); returns -1
 *
 * VARIABLES USED: string: string to search for the substring.
 *                 substring: substring we are searching for.
 *                 right_loc: right most location of the
 *                            substring in the string.
 *                 i, j, k: indices into the character strings.
 *
 * PSEUDO CODE:  assign right_loc -1 in case the substring
 *               is not found
 *
 *               initialize i to 0
 *
 *               while (string[i] is not NULL)
 *               assign j the value in i and begin looking
 *               for the substring at that point
 *
 *               assign k the value 0
 *
 *               while (string[j] equals substring[k])
 *                 if (substring[k + 1] == NULL)
 *                   assign right_loc the value in i
 *                   since the substring exists
 *                 else
 *                   increment j, and k
 *
 *               return (right_loc)  /* -1 if the substring was
```

```
 *
 *                               not found in the string */
 *
 */

str_right_index (string, substring)
   char string[];
   char substring[];      /* substring we are searching for */
{
   int i, j, k;
   int right_loc = -1;  /* right most location of the substring */

   for (i = 0; string[i] != NULL; i++)
     for (j = i, k = 0; substring[k] == string[j]; k++, j++)
       if (substring[k+1] == NULL)
          {
            right_loc = i;        /* the substring was found */
            break;                /* start looking for the
                                     next occurrence */
          }

  return (right_loc);          /* -1 if the substring was not found */
}
```

```
/*
 * NAME:    strings_are_equal (string1, string2)
 *
 * FUNCTION: Compares two strings and returns 1 if the strings
 *           are equal, and 0 if the strings are not equal.
 *
 * EXAMPLES:  strings_are_equal ("THIS IS", "IT");         returns 0
 *            strings_are_equal ("THIS IS", "THIS IS"); returns 1
 *
 * VARIABLES USED: string1, string2: strings to compare for equality.
 *                 index: index into the character strings.
 *
 * PSEUDO CODE: initialize index to 0
 *
 *              while (string1[index] equals string2[index])
 *              if (string1[index] equals NULL)
 *                  return (1) -- because the strings are equal
 *              else
 *                  increment index to point to the next letter
 *                  in each string
 *
 *              if (strings aren't equal)
 *                  return (0)
 *
 */

strings_are_equal (string1, string2)
   char string1[];
   char string2[];
 {
   int index;
```

```
   for (index = 0; string1[index] == string2[index]; index++)
      if (string1[index] == NULL)
         return (1);                /* the strings are equal */

   return (0);                      /* the strings are not equal */
}
```

```
/*
 * NAME: greater_string (string1, string2)
 *
 * FUNCTION: Returns the greater string based upon the ASCII
 *           collating sequence.  If string1 is greater, 1 is
 *           returned.  If string2 is greater, 2 is returned,
 *           and if the strings are equal 0 is returned.
 *
 * EXAMPLES: greater_string ("This", "That");      returns 1
 *           greater_string ("This", "This");      returns 0
 *           greater_string ("This is", "This"); returns 1
 *
 * VARIABLES USED: string1, string2: the strings to compare.
 *                 index: index into the character strings.
 *
 * PSEUDO CODE: initialize index to 0
 *
 *              while (string1[index] and string2[index]
 *                     aren't equal to NULL)
 *
 *                 if (string1[index] > string2[index])
 *                    return (1)
 *                 else if (string1[index] < string2[index])
 *                    return (2)
 *                 else
 *                    increment index to point to the next letter
 *                    in each string
 *
 *              if (string1[index] == string2[index])
 *                 return (0)  -- both equal NULL (i.e. same length)
 *
 *              else if (string1[index] is NULL)
 *                 return (2)  -- string2 is longer
 *
 *              else
 *                 return (1)  -- string1 is longer
 *
 */
   greater_string (string1, string2)
      char string1[];
      char string2[];
    {
      int index;
```

```
/* since we need to examine the strings until they are not
 * equal or until they equal NULL, we can use the logical  AND &&.
 *
 * if either string is NULL, (the Boolean FALSE) the logical AND
 * will terminate the loop.
 */

for (index = 0; string1[index] && string2[index]; index++)
    if (string1[index] > string2[index])
        return (1);

    else if (string1[index] < string2[index])
        return (2);

if (string1[index] == string2[index])
    return (0);                          /* strings are equal */

else if (string1[index] == NULL)
    return (2);                          /* string2 is longer */

else
    return (1);                          /* string1 is longer */
}
```

```
/*
 * NAME: remove_blanks (string)
 *
 * FUNCTION: Removes all of the blanks in the character string.
 *
 * EXAMPLE:   if string contains "THIS IS IT"
 *            remove_blanks (string); ==> THISISIT
 *
 * VARIABLES USED: string: character string to examine for blanks.
 *                 temp: temporary character string.
 *                 index_temp: index into the temporary string.
 *                 index: index into the character string.
 *
 * ROUTINES CALLED: copy_string(); copies the first string specified
 *                                 to the second string.
 *
 * MACROS USED: is_blank();   returns 1 if the character is a blank
 *                            otherwise 0 is returned.
 *
 * PSEUDO CODE: initialize index to 0
 *              initialize index_temp to 0
 *
 *              while (string[index] is not NULL)
 *                if (string[index] is not a blank)
 *                   assign it to temp[index_temp]
 *                   increment index_temp
 *                else
 *                   ignore it
 *
```

```
*                     increment index to point to the next letter
*
*                 copy the contents of the temporary string
*                 back to the string
*
*/

remove_blanks (string)
  char string[];
  {
  int index, index_temp;

  char temp[MAX_STRING];

  /* remove any blanks in the string */

  for (index = 0, index_temp = 0; string[index] != NULL; index++)
    if (is_blank(string[index]) == FALSE)
      temp [index_temp++] = string [index];

  temp[index_temp] = NULL;

  copy_string (temp, string); /* put the string with the blanks */
                              /* removed back into string */
  }
```

```
/*
* NAME: char_index (string, letter)
*
* FUNCTION: Returns the first occurrence of the character contained
*           in the variable letter within the character string, or -1
*           if the letter was not present.
*
* EXAMPLES: char_index ("THIS IS IT", 'I'); returns 2
*           char_index ("THIS IS IT", 'i'); returns -1
*
* VARIABLES USED: string: character string to search.
*                 letter: character to search for.
*                 index: index into the character string.
*
* PSEUDO CODE:  while (string[index] is not NULL)
*                   if (string[index] is equal to letter)
*                       return (index) -- location of the letter
*
*                   increment index to point to the next letter
*
*                   return (-1) since the character was not found
*
*/

char_index (string, letter)
  char string[];
  char letter;
  {
```

```
    int index;

    for (index = 0; string[index] != NULL; index++)
      if (string[index] == letter)
        return (index);

    return (-1);    /* if the character was found in the string, the
                       return statement above will return the location
                       of the character in the string, if it was not
                       found, we will return -1 */
}
```

Pointers

A pointer references a location in memory (not the value contained within the memory location). A pointer to a variable is created as follows:

```
variable_type    *variable_name;
```

To assign the pointer an address of a memory location, the ampersand (&) is used as follows:

```
int *int_ptr;              /* declare the pointer */
int_ptr = &int_variable; /* assign the address
                            of int_variable */
```

To access the value contained in the location referenced by the pointer, the asterisk (*) is used:

```
*int_ptr = 5;
```

The following code segment assigns the value 5 to the variable **a**.

```
int a = 5;
```

The next segment assigns the memory location of **a** to **int _ ptr**.

```
/* assign int_ptr the memory location of a */
int int_ptr = &a;

if (a == *int_ptr)
  printf ("Values are equal.\n");
```

The expression **if (a == *int _ ptr)** evaluates as **TRUE** since **a** and ***int _ ptr** refer to the same value.

All pointers use two values to manipulate variables and the values they contain. The first is the actual value contained in the location referenced by the pointer. The second is the **lvalue**, the location in memory of the variable or value referenced.

The following routine declares a variable of type **int** and a pointer to the variable. The variable is incremented from 1 to 10, and the **address** and **contents** of the variable are written to the screen. In addition, the contents of the pointer and the value contained in the location referenced by the pointer are also displayed:

```
/*
 * NAME: lvalue demo
 *
 * FUNCTION: Displays a variable's lvalue and value, and in
 *           addition, illustrates pointer manipulation.
 *
 * VARIABLES USED: integer_value: contains the integer value which is
 *                                incremented in the loop.
 *                 int_ptr: points to the integer value.
 *
 * PSEUDO CODE:   assign int_ptr the location in memory of
 *                integer_value
 *
 *                for (integer_value = 1 to 10)
 *                  print the address and value of integer_value
 *                  print the contents of and the location referenced
 *                  by int_ptr
 *
 */
main ()
{
  int integer_value;

  int *int_ptr = &integer_value;  /* assign memory location */

  for (integer_value = 0; integer_value <= 10; integer_value++)
    {
```

```
printf ("integer_value:value%d lvalue %x\n",
        integer_value, &integer_value);
printf ("int_ptr: contents %x  value referenced %d\n",
        int_ptr, *int_ptr);
    }
}
```

Pointers are very convenient for string manipulation. For example, many of the routines presented in Chapter 3 can be implemented with pointers to character strings. One advantage of using pointers to character strings is that you are not required to dimension arrays to contain the characters. When pointers to character strings are used in functions, a pointer to the first character in the string is passed in a manner identical to that used for arrays of characters. Once the pointer is assigned to the location of the first character in the string, you can advance through the characters contained in the string by incrementing this pointer. For example, the following while loop will print the characters referenced by **string** until NULL is found:

```
while (*string)
  putchar(*string++);
```

If **string** points to the character string "Computer", the loop will print the characters of the **string** in sequential order beginning with **string+0** and ending with the NULL character at **string+8**.

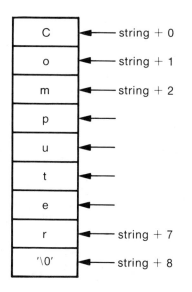

Several of the following routines have the same names as the routines presented in Chapter 3 since they perform the same function. The differences in implementation are significant and worthy of careful study.

```
/*
 * NAME: string_length (string)
 *
 * FUNCTION: Returns the number of characters contained
 *           in the variable string.
 *
 * EXAMPLE: x = string_length (string);
 *
 * VARIABLES USED: string: pointer to the character string.
 *                 count: number of characters in the string.
 *
 * PSEUDO CODE: initialize count to 0
 *
 *              while (the letter referenced by *string is not NULL)
 *                 increment count
 *                 increment string to point to the next letter
 *
 *              return (count)
 *
 */

string_length (string)
  char *string;
 {
  int count;

  for (count = 0; *string != NULL; count++)
     string++;

  return (count);
 }
```

```
/*
 * NAME: copy_string (string1, string2)
 *
 * FUNCTION: Copies string1 to string2.
 *
 * EXAMPLE: copy_string ("This is it", string2);
 *
 * VARIABLES: string1: pointer to the string being copied.
 *            string2: pointer to the destination string of
 *                     the copy.
 *
 * PSEUDO CODE: while (*string2 is replaced by the letter in
 *                     *string1 and the letter assigned is not NULL)
```

```
*              increment string1 and string2
*
*              return
*/

copy_string (string1, string2)
  char *string1;                /* string being copied */
  char *string2;
 {

  while (*string2++ = *string1++)
      ;

 /* the while loop will assign the letter contained in *string1
  * to *string2 and then test the value assigned.  If the value
  * assigned is NULL (the Boolean FALSE) the loop will terminate.
  */

 }
```

```
/*
 * NAME: append_string (string1, string2)
 *
 * FUNCTION: Appends the contents of string1 to string2.
 *
 * EXAMPLE:   if string contains "THIS IS "
 *            append_string ("IT", string); => THIS IS IT
 *
 * VARIABLES USED: string1: pointer to the string to be appended.
 *                 string2: pointer to the string appended to.
 *
 * PSEUDO CODE: while (the letter referenced by *string2 is not NULL)
 *                 increment string2 -- until the end of the string
 *
 *                 while (*string2 is assigned letter contained in
 *                     *string1 and the letter assigned is not NULL)
 *                 increment string1
 *                 increment string2
 *
 *                 return
 *
 */

append_string (string1, string2)
  char *string1;                /* string to append */
  char *string2;
 {
  /* find the end of string2 */

  while (*string2)
    string2++;
```

```
/* append the contents of string1 */

while (*string2++ = *string1++)
      ;
}
```

```
/*
 * NAME: string_comp (string1, string2)
 *
 * FUNCTION: Returns the location in string1 of the first
 *           character which is not equal to the corresponding
 *           character in string2, or the value -1 if the strings
 *           are equal.
 *
 * EXAMPLES: string_comp ("THIS", "is");    returns 0
 *           string_comp ("This", "This"); returns -1
 *
 * VARIABLES USED: string1, string2: pointers to the strings to compare.
 *                 location: location of the first difference.
 *
 * PSEUDO CODE:  initialize location to 0
 *
 *                while (*string1 == *string2)
 *                  if (*string1 == NULL)
 *                     return (-1)         -- equal strings
 *                  else
 *                     increment string1
 *                     increment string2
 *                     increment location
 *
 *                return (location)  -- first difference
 *
 */
string_comp (string1, string2)
  char *string1;
  char *string2;
 {
  int location; /* location of the first difference */

  for (location = 0; *string1 == *string2; ++location)
     if (*string1++ == NULL)
       return (-1);
     else
       string2++;

  return (location);    /* if the strings are equal, -1 is
                            is returned above. */
 }
```

```
/*
 * NAME: char_count (string, letter)
 *
 * FUNCTION: Returns the count of occurrences of the character
 *           contained in letter within the string, or 0 if the
 *           letter was not found.
 *
 * EXAMPLES: x = char_index ("THIS IS", 'J');  returns 0
 *           x = char_index ("This", 'i');      returns 1
 *
 * VARIABLES USED: string: pointer to the string to examine.
 *                 letter: contains the character we are searching for.
 *                 count: number of occurrences of the letter
 *                        in the string.
 *
 * PSEUDO CODE:   initialize count to 0
 *
 *                while (*string is not NULL)
 *                if (*string equals letter)
 *                   increment count
 *
 *                increment string to point to the next letter
 *
 *                return (count)
 *
 */
char_count (string, letter)
  char *string;
  char letter;
 {
  int count = 0;

  while (*string != NULL)
    if (*string++ == letter)
      count++;                 /* increment count and continue */
                               /* looking for the next occurrence */

  return (count);  /* number of occurrences */
 }
```

```
/*
 * NAME: right_index (string, letter)
 *
 * FUNCTION: Returns the right most location of the character
 *           contained in letter within the string, or -1 if the
 *           letter was not found.
 *
 * EXAMPLES: x = right_index ("THIS IS", 'J');  returns -1
 *           x = right_index ("This is", 'i');  returns 5
 *
```

```
*  VARIABLES USED: string: pointer to the string to examine.
*                  letter: contains the character we are
*                          searching for.
*                  rlocation: location of the right most
*                             occurrence of the character
*                             in the string.
*                  location: current location in the string.
*
*  PSEUDO CODE:  initialize rlocation to -1 in case the letter
*                            is not found
*                initialize location to 0
*
*                while (*string is not NULL)
*                if (*string equals letter)
*                  assign location to rlocation
*
*                increment string to point to the next letter
*                increment location
*
*                return (rlocation)   -- -1 is returned if the
*                                        letter was not found
*
*/

right_index (string, letter)
  char *string;
  char letter;
  {
  int rlocation = -1;   /* -1 in case the letter is not found */
  int location;

  for (location = 0; *string != NULL; location++)
    if (*string++ == letter)
      rlocation = location;

  return (rlocation);   /* right most location of the letter */

                        /* -1 is returned if the letter was */
                        /* not found                        */
  }
```

```
/*
*  NAME: char_index (string, letter)
*
*  FUNCTION: Returns the location of the first occurrence of the
*            character contained in letter within the string, or -1
*            if the letter was not found.
*
*  EXAMPLES: x = char_index ("THIS IS", 'J');  returns -1
*            x = char_index ("This", 'i');     returns 2
*
*  VARIABLES USED: string: pointer to the string to examine.
*                  letter: contains the character we are searching for.
*                  location: location of the character in the string.
*
```

```
*  PSEUDO CODE:   initialize location to 0
*
*                 while (*string is not NULL)
*                 if (*string equals letter)
*                    return (location)
*
*                 else
*                    increment string to point to the next letter
*                    increment location
*
*                 return (-1) -- letter was not found
*
*/

char_index (string, letter)
  char *string;
  char letter;
 {
  int location;

  for (location = 0; *string != NULL; location++)
    if (*string++ == letter)
      return (location);

  return (-1);   /* letter was not found. if the letter is found */
                 /* the actual character location in the string  */
                 /* is returned above                            */
 }
```

```
/*
 * NAME: replace_character (string, old_char, new_char)
 *
 * FUNCTION: Replaces each occurrence of the character contained
 *           in the variable old_char with the letter contained
 *           in new_char.
 *
 * EXAMPLE: replace_character (string, 'a', 'A');
 *
 * VARIABLES USED:  string: contains the string to examine.
 *                  old_char: contains the character to replace.
 *                  new_char: contains the character to replace the
 *                            character in old_char with.
 *
 * PSEUDO CODE: while (the character contained in *string is not NULL)
 *                 if (the character is equal to old_char)
 *                    replace the character with the contents of new_char
 *
 *                 increment string to point to the next character
 *
 *              return
 */

replace_character (string, old_char, new_char)
  char *string;
```

```
char old_char;  /* character to replace */
char new_char;  /* character to replace the old character with */
{
 while (*string)
  {
    if (*string == old_char)
       *string = new_char;

    string++;
  }
}
```

C H A P T E R

Input/Output Routines

One of the most important aspects of any programming task is the interface between the user and the program. A great deal of development time is spent on routines that get data from and supply information to the user in a meaningful form.

Although most programs require specific input and output (I/O) formats, many of the routines used to provide these formats are common to most applications. Once you have created a *good* I/O routine, it should be placed into a library of routines for use with other applications.

I/O routines must be capable of handling bad data from the user in a consistent manner. If the function prompts the user for an integer value and the user enters a character string, the routine should validate the entry and reprompt the user for the correct data.

Many programmers develop routines with this capability and then restrict the function to a specific task by hardcoding prompts such as

```
printf("Enter the number of student test scores\n");
```

Rather than restricting the routine in this fashion, the programmer should allow the prompt to be passed to the routine:

```
prompt_int (prompt);
  char *prompt;
 {
  int result;

  printf ("%s\n",prompt);

  /* remainder of the routine */
 }
```

When developing I/O routines, remember that *good* I/O routines require *good* documentation. The routines in this text use a consistent documentation format that is helpful to an individual examining the routines. In addition to including this internal documentation, an important and often overlooked step is to place the routine into a library. If you work in a programming shop, placing your routine into a library allows other programmers to access it. If you have a personal computer, a library keeps your routines organized so you don't end up with the same functions on several disks. By keeping track of the routines that are kept in the library, the number of duplicate routines is decreased substantially.

Many C compilers, especially microcomputer compilers, buffer all of the input and output performing the actual data transfer when the buffer is full, or when a **newline** (\n) character is received. The routines **inchar( )** and **console__write( )** bypass the buffer and allow the user to perform direct I/O to the terminal. Many compilers store the definitions required for console I/O in the file **conio.h**. The routines in this chapter that utilize the direct I/O features have been defined in Chapter 2 to limit the number of changes required to use the I/O tools under a different compiler. If you examine the contents of **defn.h**, you will find that there are only two definitions associated with console I/O.

```
/*
 * NAME: read_char ()
 *
 * FUNCTION: Reads a character entered from the keyboard and
 *           deletes the contents of the I/O buffer.  If your
 *           routine prompts for 2 characters in a row with
 *           getchar(), the second character returned is the
 *           the carriage return for the first input.  For
 *           example:
 *
 *           x = getchar();
 *           y = getchar();
 *
 *           x is assigned the character entered, however the
 *           carriage return is still in the input buffer and
 *           is assigned to y.  read_char() destroys the
 *           contents of the input buffer before returning.
 *
 *           If EOF occurs, read_char() returns the value EOF.
 *
 * EXAMPLES: x = read_char ();
 *           y = read_char ();
 *
 * VARIABLES USED: letter: letter returned to the calling routine.
 *                 buffer: buffer for the garbage data read.
 *
 * PSEUDO CODE:  read the character entered
 *               while (the input buffer has data)
 *                  use getchar() to read and ignore it
 *
 *               return (letter)
 *
 */

read_char ()
 {
  int letter;    /* letter returned to the calling routine */
  int buffer;    /* data remaining in the input buffer is read
                    into buffer */

  letter = getchar();  /* get the response */
  buffer = letter;

  /* get characters until the input buffer is empty */

  while (buffer != EOL && buffer != EOF)
     buffer = getchar();

  return ((buffer != EOF) ? letter : EOF);
 }
```

```
/*
 * NAME: writeln (string)
 *
 * FUNCTION: Writes the string to stdout insuring that only one
 *           newline character is written.  If a line is read
 *           from a file, we have no way of knowing whether
 *           or not it contains a newline character.  If we
 *           assume it does, and none are present, the output
 *           will consist of one long line.  If we assume it
 *           doesn't and it does, each line is double spaced.
 *           writeln() eliminates this problem.
 *
 * EXAMPLE: writeln (string);
 *
 * VARIABLES USED: string: pointer to the string to be written.
 *
 * PSEUDO CODE: while (the letter referenced by *string is not an
 *                     End of Line (EOL) AND not NULL)
 *                  print the letter
 *                  increment string to point to the next letter
 *
 *              write a newline character
 *
 */

writeln (string)
  char *string;
 {

   while (*string != EOL && *string != NULL)
     putchar(*string++);

   putchar(NEWLINE);

 }
```

_____

```
/*
 * NAME: console_write (string)
 *
 * FUNCTION: Writes the string to the console insuring that a newline
 *           character is not written.  Most compilers provide several
 *           definitions for console I/O which are normally placed
 *           in the file conio.h (console I/O).  The identifier
 *           print_char has been defined in the file defn.h to the
 *           correct console I/O routine.
 *
 * EXAMPLE: console_write ("Enter date =>");
 *
 * VARIABLES USED: string: pointer to the string to be written.
 *
 * PSEUDO CODE: while (the letter referenced by *string is not an
 *                     End of Line (EOL) or equal to NULL)
```

```
*                     print the letter
*                     increment string to point to the next letter
*
*             return without printing a newline character
*
*/

console_write (string)
  char *string;
 {

  while (*string != EOL && *string != NULL)
    print_char(*string++);  /* see defn.h for the definition */
                            /* of print_char() */
 }
```

```
/*
 * NAME: fwrite (file_pointer, string)
 *
 * FUNCTION: Writes the string to the file specified by
 *           file_pointer insuring that a newline character
 *           is not written.
 *
 * EXAMPLE: fwrite (fp, last_name);
 *
 * VARIABLES USED: string: pointer to the string to be written.
 *                 file_pointer: pointer to the output file.
 *
 * PSEUDO CODE: while (the letter referenced by *string is not an
 *                 End of Line (EOL) or equal to NULL)
 *
 *                 write the letter to the file
 *                 increment string to point to the next letter
 *
 *             return without printing a carriage return
 *
 */

fwrite (file_pointer, string)
  char *string;
  FILE *file_pointer;  /* requires stdio.h to be #included */
 {

  while (*string != EOL && *string != NULL)
    putc(*string++, file_pointer);

 }
```

```
/*
 * NAME: fwriteln (file_pointer, string)
 *
 * FUNCTION: Writes the string to the file referenced
 *           by file_pointer insuring that only one newline
 *           character is written.  If a line is read
 *           from a file, we have no way of knowing whether
 *           or not it contains a newline character.  If we
 *           assume it does, and none are present the output
 *           will consist of one long line.  If we assume it
 *           doesn't and it does, each line is double spaced.
 *           fwriteln() eliminates this problem.
 *
 * EXAMPLE: fwriteln (file_pointer, address);
 *
 * VARIABLES USED: string: pointer to the string to be written.
 *                 file_pointer: pointer to the output file.
 *
 * PSEUDO CODE: while (letter referenced by *string is not an
 *                     End of Line (EOL) OR equal to NULL)
 *                  write the letter to the file
 *                  increment string to point to the next letter
 *
 *              write a newline character to the file
 *
 */
fwriteln (file_pointer, string)
  char *string;
  FILE *file_pointer;  /* requires stdio.h be #included */
  {

  while (*string != EOL && *string != NULL)
    putc(*string++, file_pointer);

  putc(NEWLINE, file_pointer);

  }
```

```
/*
 * NAME: read_string (string)
 *
 * FUNCTION: Reads a string entered by the user and replaces
 *           the carriage return with NULL.  If end of file
 *           occurs, read_string() returns the value EOF; otherwise,
 *           read_string() returns the value NO_ERROR.
 *
 * EXAMPLE: read_string (street_address);
 *
 * VARIABLES USED: string: pointer to the string read from the user.
 *                 letter: buffer used to store the letter input. A
 *                         variable of type char is unable to store
 *                         -1 returned from getchar() when an end of
 *                         file occurs.  letter allows us to test for
 *                         this condition.
 *
```

```
* PSEUDO CODE:    while (the letter entered is not a carriage return
*                        or end of file)
*                     place the letter in the string
*                     increment string for the next letter
*
*                 assign the last character in the string to NULL
*
*                 if (end of file occurred)
*                   return (EOF)
*                 else
*                   return (NO_ERROR)
*
*/

read_string (string)
  char *string;
 {
  int letter;

  while ((letter = getchar()) != EOL && letter != EOF)
   *string++ = letter;

  *string = NULL;  /* replace carriage return with NULL */

  return ((letter == EOF) ? EOF : NO_ERROR);
 }
```

```
/*
 * NAME: readln (string)
 *
 * FUNCTION: Reads a string entered by the user and appends NULL.
 *           The carriage return remains in the string.  If end of
 *           file occurs, readln() returns the value EOF; otherwise,
 *           readln() returns the value NO_ERROR.
 *
 * EXAMPLE: readln (state);
 *
 * VARIABLES USED: string: pointer to the string read from the user.
 *                 letter: used to buffer the data input. A variable
 *                         of type char is unable to contain the -1
 *                         returned by getchar() when an end of file
 *                         occurs.  letter allows us to test for this
 *                         condition.
 *
 * PSEUDO CODE:    while (the letter entered is not a carriage return or
 *                        end of file)
 *                     place the letter in the string
 *                     increment string for the next character
 *
 *                 assign a carriage return to the string
 *                 assign the last character in the string to NULL
 *
 *                 if (end of file occurred)
 *                   return (EOF)
```

```
*               else
*                   return (NO_ERROR)
*
*/

readln (string)
  char *string;
 {
  int letter;  /* buffer used to test for EOF */

  while ((letter = getchar()) != EOL && letter != EOF)
    *string++ = letter;

  *string = NULL;  /* append NULL */

  return ((letter == EOF) ? EOF: NO_ERROR);
 }
```

```
/*
 * NAME: prompt_response (prompt, response)
 *
 * FUNCTION: Prompts the user for a response, validates and returns
 *           a character string containing the response.  If end of
 *           file occurs, prompt_response() returns EOF; otherwise,
 *           prompt_response() returns NO_ERROR.
 *
 * EXAMPLE: prompt_response ("Enter your street address", address);
 *
 * VARIABLES USED: prompt: pointer to the string containing
 *                         the prompt.
 *                 response: pointer to the string containing
 *                           the user's response.
 *                 not_valid: Boolean value to control the loop.
 *                 letter: contains Y or N response.
 *
 * ROUTINES CALLED: read_char();  reads a character.
 *                  char_index(); searches for a character in a
 *                                string.
 *                  writeln ();   writes a string and insures that
 *                                only one newline character is written.
 *
 * PSEUDO CODE:    while (the response is not valid)
 *                     prompt the user for a response
 *                     get the response
 *                     validate the response
 *
 *                 return (valid response)
 *
 */

  prompt_response (prompt, response)
    char *prompt;
    char *response;
```

```
{
 int not_valid = TRUE;        /* FALSE when the response is valid */
 int letter;                  /* letter read from the user for Y
                                 or N response */

 while (not_valid)
   {
    writeln (prompt);                          /* prompt the user */

    if (read_string (response) == EOF)
      return (EOF);

    printf ("Is %s correct? (Y/N)\n", response);    /* validate */

    if ((letter = read_char()) == EOF)
      return (EOF);

    if (char_index ("Yy", letter) != -1)
      not_valid = FALSE;
   }
   return (NO_ERROR);
  }
```

```
/*
 * NAME: get_response (response)
 *
 * FUNCTION: Obtains a response from the user, validates and returns
 *           the character string containing the response.  If end of
 *           file occurs, get_response() returns the value EOF; otherwise
 *           get_response() returns NO_ERROR.
 *
 * EXAMPLE: get_response (last_name);
 *
 * VARIABLES USED: response: pointer to the string containing
 *                           the user's response.
 *                 not_valid: Boolean value to control the loop.
 *                 letter: contains Y or N response.
 *
 * ROUTINES CALLED: read_char();  reads a character.
 *                  char_index(); searches for a character in a
 *                                string.
 *
 * PSEUDO CODE:     while (the response is not valid)
 *                     get the response
 *                     validate the response
 *                     if (the response is not valid)
 *                        ask user to enter a new response
 *
 *                  return (valid response)
 *
 */

get_response (response)
  char *response;
```

```
{
  int not_valid = TRUE;        /* FALSE when the response is valid */
  int letter;                  /* letter read from the user for Y
                                  or N response */

  while (not_valid)
    {
     if (read_string (response) == EOF)      /* get the response */
       return (EOF);

     printf ("Is %s correct? (Y/N)\n", response);   /* validate */

     letter = read_char();

     if (char_index ("Yy", letter) != -1)
       not_valid = FALSE;

     else
       printf ("Enter correct response.\n");
    }
  return (NO_ERROR);
}
```

```
/*
 * NAME: prompt_int (prompt)
 *
 * FUNCTION: Prompts the user to enter an integer value, validates
 *           the value and returns it to the calling routine.  If
 *           the user continues to enter invalid data, the routine
 *           will continue to prompt the user for correct data. If
 *           EOF occurs, prompt_int() returns the value 0.
 *
 * EXAMPLE: x = prompt_int ("Enter your age");
 *
 * VARIABLES USED: prompt: pointer to the string containing the prompt.
 *                 result: contains the valid integer.
 *                 not_valid: Boolean value to control the loop.
 *                 ascii_val: the ASCII value entered by the user.
 *
 * ROUTINES CALLED: int_convert (); converts an ASCII string to an
 *                                   integer value.
 *                  writeln(); writes a string and insures only
 *                             one newline character is written.
 *
 * PSEUDO CODE:  while (data is not valid)
 *                   prompt the user for an integer value
 *                   get the data
 *                   validate the data
 *                   if (the data is not valid)
 *                     display an error message
 *
 *               once the data is valid
 *                   return (result)
 *
 */
```

```
prompt_int (prompt)
  char *prompt;
 {
  int not_valid = TRUE;  /* FALSE when a valid integer is entered  */
  int result;            /* value to return to the calling routine */
  char ascii_val[MAX_STRING];        /* data entered by the user */

  while (not_valid)
   {
    writeln (prompt);                      /* prompt the user */

    if (read_string (ascii_val) == EOF)      /* get the input */
      return (0);

    /* convert the string to the corresponding integer value */

    if (int_convert (ascii_val, &result) == NO_ERROR)
      not_valid = FALSE;

    else
      printf ("Invalid data entered.  Enter integer value.\n");
   }

    return (result);  /* valid integer value */
  }
```

```
/*
 * NAME: get_integer ()
 *
 * FUNCTION: Returns a valid integer value without prompting user.
 *           If end of file occurs, get_integer() returns the value 0.
 *
 * EXAMPLE: x = get_integer ();
 *
 * VARIABLES USED:  not_valid: Boolean value to control the loop.
 *                  result: value returned to the calling routine.
 *                  ascii_val: the ASCII value entered by the user.
 *
 * ROUTINES CALLED: int_convert(); converts an ASCII string to
 *                                  an integer value.
 *
 * PSEUDO CODE: while (the data entered is not valid)
 *                 get the new data
 *                 validate the data
 *                 if (the data is not valid)
 *                    display an error message
 *
 *              return (valid result)
 *
 */

get_integer ()
  {
   int not_valid = TRUE;   /* FALSE when the data is valid */
   int result;             /* value returned to the calling routine */
```

```
    char ascii_val[MAX_STRING];     /* data entered by the user */

  while (not_valid)
    {
      if (read_string (ascii_val) == EOF)        /* get the data */
        return (0);

      /* convert the string to the corresponding integer value */

      if (int_convert (ascii_val, &result) == NO_ERROR)
        not_valid = FALSE;

      else
          printf ("Invalid data entered.  Enter integer value.\n");
    }

  return (result);    /* valid integer value */
}
```

```
/*
 * NAME: int_convert (ascii_val, result)
 *
 * FUNCTION: Converts the ASCII representation of a number
 *           to the actual decimal value.  If an error
 *           occurs IO_ERROR is returned.
 *
 * EXAMPLE: result = int_convert (ascii_val);
 *
 * VARIABLES USED:  ascii_val: pointer to the string containing
 *                             ASCII representation of a value.
 *                  sign: positive or negative.
 *                  result: value desired.
 *
 * MACROS USED: is_blank(); returns 1 if the letter is a blank
 *                          otherwise 0
 *              is_digit(); returns 1 if the letter is a  digit
 *                          otherwise 0
 *              to_decimal(); returns decimal value represented
 *                            by the ASCII character.
 *
 * PSEUDO CODE:   while (the letter referenced by *ascii_val is a blank)
 *                    increment ascii_val to skip blanks
 *
 *                if (the sign of the value is present)
 *                    determine if positive or negative
 *                    increment ascii_val to point to the
 *                        next character
 *                else
 *                    assume the value is positive
 *
 *                while (the letter in *ascii_val is not NULL)
 *                  if (the letter is a digit)
 *                      convert the letter to decimal
 *
```

```
*                     multiply the previous value contained in
*                     result by 10 to obtain correct 10s place
*
*                     add the new value to result
*
*                 else if (the letter is not a digit)
*                     return (IO_ERROR)  -- invalid character
*
*                 increment ascii_val to point to the next digit
*
*                 return (NO_ERROR);
*
*/

int_convert (ascii_val, result)
  char *ascii_val;
  int *result;
 {
   int sign = 1;   /* -1 if negative */

   *result = 0;    /* value returned to the calling routine */

   /* read passed blanks */

   while (is_blank(*ascii_val))
       ascii_val++;                    /* get the next letter */

   /* check for sign */

   if (*ascii_val == '-' || *ascii_val == '+')
       sign = (*ascii_val++ == '-') ? -1 : 1;  /* determine the sign */
                                               /* increment ascii_val */
   /*
    * convert the ASCII representation to the actual
    * decimal value by subtracting '0' from each character.
    *
    * for example, the ASCII '9' is equivalent to 57 in decimal.
    * by subtracting '0' (or 48 in decimal) we get the desired
    * value.
    *
    * if we have already converted '9' to 9 and the next character
    * is '3', we must first multiply 9 by 10 and then convert '3'
    * to decimal and add it to the previous total yielding 93.
    *
    */

   while (*ascii_val)
    if (is_digit(*ascii_val))
      *result = *result * 10 + to_decimal(*ascii_val++);

    else
      return (IO_ERROR);

   *result = *result * sign;

   return (NO_ERROR);
}
```

```
/*
 * NAME: prompt_float (prompt)
 *
 * FUNCTION: Prompts the user for a floating point value, validates
 *           the value and returns it to the calling routine.  If
 *           the user enters an invalid value, the routine continues
 *           to prompt the user until valid data is entered.  If end
 *           of file occurs, prompt_float() returns the value 0.0
 *
 * EXAMPLE: x = prompt_float ("Enter percentage of graduates.");
 *
 * VARIABLES USED: prompt: pointer to the string containing the
 *                         prompt.
 *                 result: contains the value returned to the
 *                         calling routine.
 *                 not_valid: Boolean value to control the loop.
 *                 ascii_val: the ASCII value entered by the user.
 *
 * ROUTINES CALLED: float_convert(); converts an ASCII string to
 *                                   a floating point value.
 *                  writeln (); writes a string and insures only
 *                              one newline character is written.
 *
 * PSEUDO CODE: while (the data is not valid)
 *                  prompt the user for a floating point value
 *                  get the new data
 *                  validate the data
 *                  if (the data is not valid)
 *                      display an error message
 *
 *              return (valid result)
 *
 */

float prompt_float (prompt)
  char *prompt;
{
  int not_valid = TRUE;      /* FALSE when the data entered is valid  */

  float result;              /* value returned to the calling routine */

  char ascii_val[MAX_STRING];           /* data entered by the user */

  while (not_valid)
    {
      writeln (prompt);                 /* prompt the user for a value */

      if (read_string (ascii_val) == EOF)   /* read the value entered */
        return (0.0);

      /* convert the string to the corresponding floating point value */

      if (float_convert (ascii_val, &result) == NO_ERROR)
          not_valid = FALSE;
```

```
        else
            writeln ("Invalid data entered.  Enter type float.\n");
    }

    return (result);    /* valid floating point value */
}
```

```
/*
 * NAME: get_float ()
 *
 * FUNCTION: Returns a valid floating point value without prompting
 *           the user.  If end of file occurs, get_float() returns the
 *           value 0.0.
 *
 * EXAMPLE: x = get_float ();
 *
 * VARIABLES USED: result: contains the value returned to the
 *                         calling routine.
 *                 not_valid: Boolean value to control the loop.
 *                 ascii_val: pointer to the data entered by
 *                            the user.
 *
 * ROUTINES CALLED: float_convert(); converts an ASCII string to
 *                                   a floating point value.
 *
 * PSEUDO CODE: while (the data is not valid)
 *                  get the new data
 *                  validate the data
 *                  if (the data is not valid)
 *                      display an error message
 *
 *              return (valid result)
 *
 */
float get_float ()
{
    int not_valid = TRUE;     /* FALSE when the data entered is valid  */

    float result;             /* value returned to the calling routine */

    char ascii_val[MAX_STRING];          /* data entered by the user */

    while (not_valid)
    {
        if (read_string (ascii_val) == EOF)            /* get the data */
            return (0.0);

        /* convert the string to the corresponding floating point value */

        if (float_convert (ascii_val, &result) == NO_ERROR)
            not_valid = FALSE;
```

```
    else
         printf ("Invalid data entered.  Enter type float\n");
  }

 return (result);  /* valid floating point number */
}
```

```
/*
 * NAME: float_convert (ascii_val, result)
 *
 * FUNCTION: Converts the ASCII representation of a number
 *           to the actual floating point value.  If an error
 *           occurs IO_ERROR is returned.
 *
 * EXAMPLE: result = float_convert (ascii_val);
 *
 * VARIABLES USED:   ascii_val: pointer to the string containing
 *                        the ASCII representation of a value.
 *                   sign: positive or negative.
 *                   result: value desired.
 *                   count: number of digits to the right of
 *                        the decimal point.
 *
 * ROUTINES CALLED: power (value, raised_to); raises the value to
 *                                       the power specified.
 *
 * MACROS USED: is_blank(); returns 1 if the letter is a blank
 *                        otherwise 0
 *              is_digit(); returns 1 if the letter is a digit
 *                        otherwise 0
 *              to_decimal(); returns the decimal value referenced
 *                        by the ASCII character.
 *
 * PSEUDO CODE:  while (letter referenced by *ascii_val is a blank)
 *                   increment ascii_val to skip blanks
 *
 *               if (the sign of the value is present)
 *                   determine if positive or negative
 *                   increment ascii_val to point to the
 *                      next character
 *               else
 *                   assume the value is positive
 *
 *               while (the letter in *ascii_val is not NULL)
 *                if (the letter is a digit)
 *                   convert the value to decimal
 *
 *                   multiply the previous value contained in
 *                   result by 10 to obtain correct 10s place
 *                   add the new value to result
 *
 *                else if (the letter is not a digit)
 *                   if (the letter is decimal point)
 *                      break this loop
 *
```

```
*                    else
*                       return (IO_ERROR) -- invalid character
*
*                    increment ascii_val to point to the next digit
*
*               while (the letter in *ascii_val is not NULL)
*                  if (the letter is digit)
*                     convert the letter to decimal
*
*                     add the value to the appropriate decimal place
*                     by dividing by 10 raised to the count of the #
*                     number of digits to the right of the decimal point
*
*                     increment ascii_val to point to the next digit
*
*                  else
*                     return (IO_ERROR)
*
*               return (NO_ERROR)
*
*/

float_convert (ascii_val, result)
  char *ascii_val;
  float *result;
{
  int count;              /* number of digits to the right of
                             the decimal point. */
  int sign = 1;           /* -1 if negative */

  float power();          /* function returning a value raised
                             to the power specified. */

  *result = 0.0;          /* value desired by the calling routine */

  /* read passed blanks */

  while (is_blank(*ascii_val))
      ascii_val++;                 /* get the next letter */

  /* check for a sign */

  if (*ascii_val == '-' || *ascii_val == '+')
      sign = (*ascii_val++ == '-') ? -1 : 1;  /* determine the sign */
                                              /* increment ascii_val */
  /*
   * first convert the numbers on the left of the decimal point.
   *
   * if the number is 33.141592  this loop will convert 33
   *
   * convert ASCII representation to the  actual decimal
   * value by subtracting '0' from each character.
   *
   * for example, the ASCII '9' is equivalent to 57 in decimal.
   * by subtracting '0' (or 48 in decimal) we get the desired
   * value.
   *
```

```
 * if we have already converted '9' to 9 and the next character
 * is '3', we must first multiply 9 by 10 and then convert '3'
 * to decimal and add it to the previous total yielding 93.
 *
 */

while (*ascii_val)
  if (is_digit(*ascii_val))
    *result = *result * 10 + to_decimal(*ascii_val++);

  else if (*ascii_val == '.')  /* start the fractional part */
    break;

  else
    return (IO_ERROR);


/*
 * find number to the right of the decimal point.
 *
 * if the number is 33.141592 this portion will return 141592.
 *
 * by converting a character and then dividing it by 10
 * raised to the number of digits to the right of the
 * decimal place the digits are placed in the correct locations.
 *
 *     4 / power (10, 2) ==> 0.04
 *
 */

if (*ascii_val != NULL)
  {
    ascii_val++;    /* past decimal point */

    for (count = 1; *ascii_val != NULL; count++, ascii_val++)

      if (is_digit(*ascii_val))
        *result = *result + to_decimal(*ascii_val)/power(10.0,count);

      else
        return (IO_ERROR);
  }

 *result = *result * sign; /* positive or negative value */

 return (NO_ERROR);
}


/*
 * NAME: power (value, n)
 *
 * FUNCTION: raises the value contained in value to the nth power.
 *           n must be a positive value or -1 is returned.
 *
```

```
 * EXAMPLE: x = power (5, 2); assigns x the value 25.
 *
 * VARIABLES USED: value: value to raise.
 *                 n: power we are raising value to.
 *                 result: value returned.
 *                 count: count of iterations.
 *
 * PSEUDO CODE: if (n is negative)
 *                  return (-1)
 *
 *              initialize result to 1
 *              initialize count to 1
 *
 *              while (count <= n)
 *                 assign result the value of value * result
 *                 increment count
 *
 *              return (result)
 *
 */
float power (value, n)
  float value;
  int n;                /* power to raise value to */
  {
  int count;
  float result = 1.0; /* value returned */

  if (n < 0)
    return (-1.0);      /* won't take the root of a value */

  /*
   * if n = 3 and value = 5 the loop will perform the following:
   *
   * count = 1       result = 1 * 5
   * count = 2       result = 5 * 5
   * count = 3       result = 25 * 5
   *
   * return result or 125
   *
   */

  for (count = 1; count <= n ; count++)
    result = result * value;

  return (result);
  }
```

```
/*
 * NAME: non_fatal_error (error_message)
 *
 * FUNCTION: Display an error message on the screen and prompt user
 *           to hit <return> to continue.
 *
```

```
* EXAMPLE: non_fatal_error ("Invalid date entered.");
*
* VARIABLES USED: error_message: pointer to the error message.
*                 count: counter.
*
* MACROS USED: BELL;  sounds the computer bell.
*
* ROUTINES CALLED: writeln(); writes a string and insures that
*                  only one newline character is written.
*
* PSEUDO CODE: ring the computer bell
*              display the error message
*              prompt the user to hit <return>
*              wait for <return>
*
*              return
*
*/

non_fatal_error (error_message)
  char *error_message;
 {
  int count;

  for (count = 0; count < 5; count++)
    BELL;

  writeln (error_message);
  console_write ("Hit <return> to continue =>");

  /* wait for return */

  read_char ();
 }
```

```
/*
 * NAME: fatal_error (error_message)
 *
 * FUNCTION: Display an error message and exit to operating system.
 *
 * EXAMPLE: fatal_error ("Error in data.  Contact KDH");
 *
 * VARIABLES USED: error_message: pointer to the error message.
 *                 count: counter.
 *
 * MACROS USED: BELL; sounds the computer bell.
 *
 * ROUTINES USED: writeln(); writes a string and insures that
 *                only one newline character is written.
 *
 * PSEUDO CODE: sound the computer bell
 *              display an error message
 *              exit to the operating system
 *
 */
```

```
fatal_error (error_message)
  char *error_message;
  {
  int count;

  for (count = 0; count < 10; count++)  /* ring the computer bell */
    BELL;

  writeln (error_message);

  exit (1);
  }
```

```
/*
 * NAME: inchar ()
 *
 * FUNCTION: Gets a character from the user without echoing the
 *           character back to the screen, or waiting for a
 *           carriage return.  It is similar to the inchar
 *           by BASIC on most systems.  Since most I/O is buffered,
 *           inchar() and console_write() provide an alternate method
 *           via direct I/O.
 *
 *           The routines required for direct input are again accessed
 *           via the file conio.h (console i/o).  The routine inchar()
 *           uses get_character which as been assigned the proper
 *           definition in defn.h.
 *
 * EXAMPLE: letter = inchar();
 *
 * VARIABLES USED: character: character entered by the user.
 *
 * PSEUDO CODE: get the letter entered by the user
 *              if the letter is a control character
 *                   return (EOF)
 *              else
 *                   return (the letter)
 *
 */

inchar ()
  {
  int character;

  character = get_character();

  return ((is_control(character)) ? EOF : character);
  }
```

```
/* the following line of code waits for the user to enter
 * a valid y or Y to a yes or no question:
 *
```

```
* for (i = inchar(); char_index ("yY", i) == -1 ;i = inchar()) ;
*
* none of the letters entered by the user will be displayed on the
* screen.
*
*/
```

C H A P T E R

6

Array Manipulation Routines

While many C programmers feel confident with arrays and zero-based addressing because of the extensive use of arrays in string manipulation, the majority have misconceptions about the generic use of arrays in C. For example, a programmer will develop separate routines for calculating the average of an array of type **int** and the average of an array of type **float** rather than employing the tools provided by C. A major goal of developing these tools is to prevent duplication of effort. C provides a powerful tool in the #**define** statement, which can be used to limit duplicate routines.

For example, if you develop your array manipulation routines to handle data of type **array — type**, you can later use the #**define** statement to assign **array — type** the proper type:

```
#define array_type float
```

If the arrays are defined in your routines as

```
array_type array[];
```

the C preprocessor will assign the appropriate type to each array during compilation. This definition must be one of the first statements in your program if it is to be used in routines that are not contained in the source file and are included with the #**include** statement. The **typedef** statement can be used in a similar manner:

```
typedef float array_type;
```

Many of these routines perform what may appear to be minor or trivial tasks, but that is what makes them successful as tools. By breaking each task into individual functions **sum, average — value**, and so on, the readability and reusability of the routines have been increased.

Binary Search

A binary search is one of the simplest and quickest searching algorithms used by programmers. While the sequential search examines successive elements of the array, in a binary search the elements of the array are repeatedly divided in half until the desired record is found. In order for a binary search to be performed, the array *must* have been previously sorted in ascending order. For example, consider the following arrays:

EMPLOYEE	I.D. NUMBER	SALARY
PARRISH	1111	30000
FLOOD	2222	40000
BARNES	3807	20000
KEMPF	4516	25000
MOORE	6500	35000
BURKE	6770	60000
NELSON	7777	10000
BYRD	8107	80000
BROWN	8321	55000
SMITH	9909	25000

If you need to know Nelson's salary, and you know his I.D. number is 7777, you can search the array **id—number[]** sequentially for 7777, which requires seven iterations before you find the value, or you can use a binary search. The variables used in the binary search are

> **not—found: FALSE** when the desired value is found
> **low**: the lowest element in the search range
> **high**: the highest element in the search range
> **value**: the value you are searching for
> **mid**: the element to be compared to the value
> **array**: the array of values to be examined

The entire array will be examined in the first iteration of the search, so the variable **low** is assigned the value 0, and **high** is assigned **num_elements** −1. You calculate **mid**, which points to the element to be examined, as follows:

```
mid = (high + low) / 2;
```

Since you are performing integer division, the value assigned to **mid** is 4.

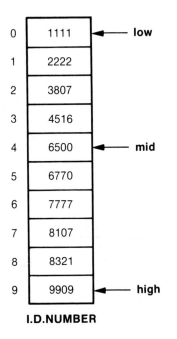

I.D.NUMBER

If the value contained in **array[mid]** == 7777, you will set the variable **not_found** to **FALSE**:

```
if (array[mid] == value)
   not_found = FALSE;
```

If the value contained in the **array[mid]** is greater than 7777, you must modify the value contained in **high** since there is no reason to search past that point in the array for 7777. For example, if the array contains

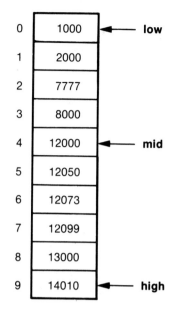

there is no reason to examine the elements contained from **mid** to **high** for the value, so you modify the value contained in **high** as follows:

```
high = mid - 1;
```

This in effect creates a new range of values to be examined for 7777.

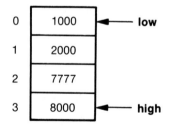

The value contained in **mid** must also be modified:

```
mid = (high + low) / 2;
```

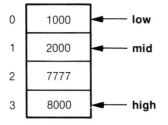

Likewise, if the initial array contains the following:

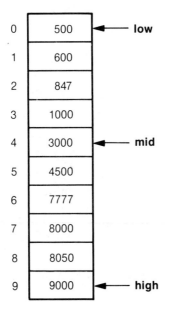

the value contained in **low** will be modified by the statement

```
if (array[mid] < value)
    low = mid + 1;
```

This statement modifies the range of values to be examined as follows:

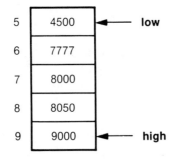

Again the value in **mid** is modified with the expression

```
mid = (high + low) / 2;
```

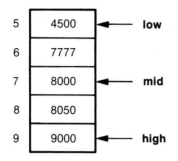

The three possible conditions can be summarized as

```
if (array[mid] == value)
  not_found = FALSE;

else if (array[mid] > value)
  high = mid - 1;

else
  low = mid + 1;

mid = (high + low) / 2;
```

Once the value is found, the variable **not ▁found** allows you to exit the loop; however, a secondary test is required in case the value you are searching for is not found. If, for example, the array contains

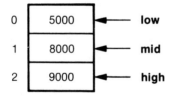

and you are searching for the value 7777, the first iteration of the search will modify the values as follows:

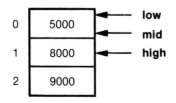

The second iteration produces

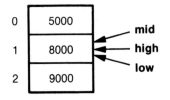

The third iteration illustrates the problem that will occur if the secondary test is not included:

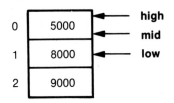

The routine will be in error since you have already examined 5000. The secondary test becomes

```
while (not_found && high >= low)
   {
     if (array[mid] == value)
       not_found = FALSE;

     else if (array[mid] > value)
        high = mid - 1;

     else
        low = mid + 1;

     mid = (high + low) / 2;
   }
```

```
/*
 * NAME: binary_search (array, num_elements, value)
 *
 * FUNCTION: Returns the location of value in the array or, -1
 *           if value is not found.  The array must be previously
 *           sorted in ascending order.
 *
```

```
 * EXAMPLE: location = binary_search (array, num_elements, value)
 *
 * VARIABLES USED: array: the array of values.
 *                 num_elements: number of elements in the array.
 *                 value: value we are searching for.
 *                 low: lowest element in the search range.
 *                 high: highest element in the search range.
 *                 mid: (high + low) / 2
 *
 * PSEUDO CODE: initialize low to 0
 *              initialize high to num_elements -1
 *              initialize mid to (high + low)/2
 *              initialize not_found to TRUE
 *
 *              while (value is not found and (high > low))
 *                 if (array[mid] equals the value)
 *                    set not_found to FALSE breaking the loop
 *
 *                 else if (array[mid] is > value)
 *                    reassign high to the value mid - 1
 *
 *                 else
 *                    reassign low to the value mid + 1
 *
 *                 reassign mid to the value (high + low) / 2
 *
 *              if (the value was not found)
 *                 return (-1)  since the value was not found
 *              else
 *                 return (mid) which is the location of the value
 *                 in the array
 *
 */

binary_search (array, num_elements, value)
  array_type array[];
  int num_elements;
  array_type value;
{
  int high = num_elements - 1;
  int low = 0;
  int mid = (high + low) / 2;

  int not_found = TRUE;

  while (not_found && high > low)
   {

   if (array[mid] == value)
     not_found = FALSE;            /* value found in the array */

   else if (array[mid] > value)
     high = mid - 1;

   else                           /* array[mid] < value */
     low = mid + 1;

   mid = (high + low) / 2;
   }
```

```
  if (not_found)
    return (-1);
  else
    return (mid);
}
```

```
/*
 * NAME: max_element (array, num_elements)
 *
 * FUNCTION: Returns the maximum value contained in an array.
 *
 * EXAMPLE: max_value = max_element (array, 12);
 *
 * VARIABLES USED: array: the array of values to examine.
 *                 index: index into the array.
 *                 num_elements: number of elements in the array.
 *                 current_maximum: current maximum value.
 *
 * MACROS USED: max(); returns the maximum of 2 values.
 *
 * PSEUDO CODE: initialize current_maximum to array[0]
 *              initialize index to 1
 *
 *              while (index < the number of elements in the array)
 *                 if (array[index] > current_maximum)
 *                    assign array[index] to current_maximum
 *                 increment index to point to the next value
 *
 *              return (current_maximum)
 *
 */
array_type max_element (array, num_elements)
  array_type array[];
  int num_elements;
 {
  array_type current_maximum = array[0]; /* assign initial value */

  int index;

  for (index = 1; index < num_elements; index++)
    current_maximum = max(array[index], current_maximum);

  return (current_maximum);
 }
```

```
/*
 * NAME: min_element (array, num_elements)
 *
 * FUNCTION: Returns the minimum value contained in an array.
 *
 * EXAMPLE: min_value = min_element (array, 12);
 *
 * VARIABLES USED: array: the array of values to examine.
 *                 index: index into the array.
 *                 num_elements: number of elements in the array.
 *                 current_minimum: current minimum value.
 *
 * MACROS USED: min(); returns the minimum of 2 values.
 *
 * PSEUDO CODE: initialize current_minimum to the value in array[0]
 *              initialize index to 1
 *
 *              while (index < the number of elements in the array)
 *                 if (array[index] < current_minimum)
 *                    assign array[index] to current_minimum
 *                 increment index to point to the next value
 *
 *              return (current_minimum)
 *
 */
array_type min_element (array, num_elements)
  array_type array[];
  int num_elements;
{
  int index;

  array_type current_minimum = array[0];  /* provide initial value */

  for (index = 1; index < num_elements; index++)
    current_minimum = min(array[index], current_minimum);

  return (current_minimum);
}
```

```
/*
 * NAME: sum (array, num_elements)
 *
 * FUNCTION: Returns the sum of the values contained in
 *           an array.
 *
 * EXAMPLE: x = sum (array, 10);
 *
```

```
 *  VARIABLES USED: array: the array of values to sum.
 *                  index: index into the array.
 *                  num_elements: number of elements in the array.
 *                  sum: value returned to the calling routine.
 *
 *  PSEUDO CODE:  initialize index and sum to 0
 *
 *                while (index < is less than the number of elements)
 *                   add the value contained in array[index] to the sum
 *                   increment index to point to the next value
 *
 *                return (sum)
 *
 */

array_type sum (array, num_elements)
  array_type array[];
  int num_elements;
{
  int index;

  array_type sum = 0.0;

  for (index = 0; index < num_elements; ++index)
    sum = sum + array[index];

  return (sum);
}
```

```
/*
 *  NAME: average_value (array, num_elements)
 *
 *  FUNCTION: Returns the average value in an array.
 *
 *  EXAMPLE: ave = average_value (array, num_elements);
 *
 *  VARIABLES USED: array: the array of values.
 *                  num_elements: number of elements in the array.
 *
 *  ROUTINES CALLED: sum(); returns the sum of the values in
 *                          the array.
 *
 *  PSEUDO CODE:  Return the sum of the elements divided by the
 *                the number of elements
 *
 */

array_type average_value (array, num_elements)
  array_type array[];
  int num_elements;
{
  array_type sum();      /* returns the sum of
                            the elements in the array */
```

```
  return (sum (array, num_elements) / num_elements);
}
```

```
/*
 * NAME: variance (array, num_elements);
 *
 * FUNCTION: Returns the variance of the values in the array.
 *
 * EXAMPLE: var = variance (array, num_elements);
 *
 * VARIABLES USED: array: the array of values.
 *                 num_elements: number of elements in the array.
 *                 ave: average value in the array.
 *                 sum: sum of the values in the array.
 *                 index: index into the array.
 *
 * MACROS USED: square(); returns the square of a value.
 *
 * PSEUDO CODE: compute the average value in the array
 *
 *              for (each element in the array)
 *                 sum the square of  (value - the average)
 *                 i.e. sum = sum + square(array[i] - average)
 *
 *              calculate variance by (sum / num_elements)
 *
 *              return (variance)
 *
 */
float variance (array, num_elements)
  array_type array[];
  int num_elements;
{
  array_type average_value ();

  int index;

  float ave;         /* average value in the array */
  float sum = 0.0;   /* sum each element - the average value */

  ave = (float) average_value (array, num_elements);

  /* compute the sum of each element - the average value */

  for (index = 0; index < num_elements; index++)
    sum = sum + square((array[index] - ave));

  return (sum / num_elements);   /* variance */
}
```

```
/*
 * NAME: standard_deviation (array, num_elements)
 *
 * FUNCTION: Returns the standard deviation of the values in
 *           the array.
 *
 * EXAMPLE: std_dev = standard_deviation (array, num_elements);
 *
 * VARIABLES USED: array: the array of values.
 *                 num_elements: number of elements in the array.
 *                 std: the standard deviation of the values in
 *                      the array.
 *                 var: the variance of the values in the array.
 *
 * ROUTINES CALLED: sqrt();     returns the square root of a value.
 *                  variance(); returns the variance of the values
 *                              in an array.
 *
 * PSEUDO CODE: compute the variance
 *              compute the standard deviation as:
 *       std = sqrt((variance * num_elements) / (num_elements - 1))
 *
 *              return (the standard deviation)
 *
 */
float standard_deviation (array, num_elements)
  array_type array[];
  int num_elements;
  {
  float var;          /* variance */
  float std;          /* standard deviation */

  float sqrt();       /* returns the square root of a value */
  float variance();   /* returns the variance of the values */
                      /* in an array */

  var = variance (array, num_elements);

  std = sqrt ((var * num_elements) / (num_elements - 1));

  return (std);
  }
```

Recursion

Many iterative procedures that at first appear difficult to develop can often be expressed in a few lines of code via recursion. A recursive function invokes itself to perform a specific task.

Many programmers avoid recursive functions because they are not comfortable with the concept or the process. This chapter will present several recursive algorithms. The importance of using debug write statements within each routine to increase your understanding of the actual processing cannot be stressed enough. Experiment with the following routines, and you will find recursion to be a powerful programming tool.

Probably the most common example of recursion is the factorial problem. For example, the factorial of 4 is defined as

```
4 * 3 * 2 * 1
```

which is really

```
4 * factorial (3)
```

Likewise, the factorial of 3 can be expressed as

```
3 * factorial (2)
```

and the factorial of 2 defined as

```
2 * factorial (1)
```

By definition, the factorial of 1 and 0 is 1. The following computes the factorial of n:

```
if (the value in n equals 0 or 1 )
    return (1) -- by definition

else
    return (n * factorial (n - 1));
```

The routine **fact( )** continues to invoke itself until an ending condition is met, which in this case is the factorial of 1. To thoroughly understand the process involved, implement the routine with the following debug write statements:

```
if (n == 1)
  {
    printf ("Returning the value 1 by definition.\n");
    return (1);
  }

else
  {
    printf ("Value received %d fact invoked with %d\n",
            n, n - 1);
    return (n * fact (n - 1));
  }
```

If the routine **fact( )** is invoked with the value 3, the following processing will occur:

```
fact (3);
  return (3 * fact (3 - 1));

    fact (2);
```

```
      return (2 * fact (2 - 1));

         fact (1);
            return (1);

      2 -- result of fact(2)

   6 -- result of fact(3)
                     .
```

The following function uses a recursive algorithm to implement the routine **power( )** from Chapter 5. If, for example, you need to find the value of 5 raised to the power of 4, **power (5, 4)**, you are really solving for

```
   5 * power (5, 3);
```

Likewise, **power (5, 3)** is equivalent to

```
   5 * power (5, 2);
```

When the power the value is raised to is equal to 0 (the ending point), the value 1 is returned to the calling routine.

If **power( )** is invoked with **power (5, 2)**, the following processing is performed:

```
power (5,2);
  return (5 * power (5, 2 - 1);

    power (5,1)
      return (5 * power (5, 1 - 1);

        power (5,0)
          return(1); -- by definition

    5 -- result of power (5,1)

25 -- result of power (5,2)
```

The following routine prints the contents of a string in reverse order. The routine is invoked with a pointer to a character string. If the pointer does not point to NULL, the routine invokes itself with ++**pointer**. If the letter equals NULL (the ending condition), the pointer is decremented and each letter referenced by the pointer is printed. For example, if the pointer **string** points to the string "Hello", the following processing is performed:

```
    print_rev (string);
      *string points to H
      print_rev(++string);
      putchar (*(--string));

        print_rev (string);
          *string points to e
          print_rev(++string);
          putchar (*(--string));

            print_rev (string);
              *string points to l
              print_rev(++string);
              putchar (*(--string));

                print_rev (string);
                  *string points to l
                  print_rev(++string);
                  putchar (*(--string));

                    print_rev (string);
                      *string points to o
                      print_rev(++string);
                      putchar (*(--string));

                        print_rev (string);
                          *string points to \0   -- ending condition
                          return();

                o

          l

      l

  e

H
```

The following routine reverses a string, or a substring contained in the string, via recursion. The routine is invoked as follows:

```
string_rev (string, starting_location, ending_location);
```

For example, assume the pointer **string** points to the string

```
"this is it"
```

To reverse the substring "is", invoke **string __rev ( )** with

```
string_rev (string 5, 6);
```

Likewise, to reverse the entire string, use **string—rev( )** as follows:

```
string_rev (string, 0, string_length (string));
```

If the variable **string** points to the string "computer" and **string—rev( )** is invoked with

```
string_rev (string, 0, string_length (string));
```

the following processing will occur:

```
string_rev (string, 0, string_length (string));
   reverses the c and r producing romputec
   string_rev (string, ++start, --end);

   string_rev (string, 1, 6);
      reverses the o and e producing remputoc
      string_rev (string, ++start, --end);

         string_rev (string, 2, 5);
            reverses the m and t producing retpumoc
            string_rev (string, ++start, --end);

            string_rev (string, 3, 4);
               reverses the p and u producing retupmoc
               string_rev (string, ++start, --end);

               string_rev (string, 4, 3);
               start >= end     returns reversed string
```

The following routine counts the number of characters contained in a string via a recursive process:

```
string_length (string);
```

The routine examines the value referenced by ***string** to see if it is NULL (the ending condition). If ***string** does not point to NULL, the value returned is

```
return (1 + string_length (++string));
```

If ***string** is NULL, the values will be returned until the actual count of the number of characters in the string is returned to the calling routine.

If the routine **string—length( )** is invoked with the string "Hello", the following processing will occur:

```
string_length (string);
 *string points to H
 return (1 + string_length (++string));


  string_length (string);
   *string points to e
   return (1 + string_length (++string));


    string_length (string);
     *string points to l
     return (1 + string_length (++string));


      string_length (string);
       *string points to l
       return (1 + string_length (++string));


        string_length (string);
         *string points to o
         return (1 + string_length (++string));


          string_length (string);
           *string points to \0
           return (0);   the ending condition
```

```
            1
          2
        3
      4
    5
```

The traditional game Towers of Hanoi is also an example of recursion. The game involves three towers; three disks are on tower A. The largest disk is on the bottom and the smallest is on the top. The object is to move all of the disks to tower B by moving one disk at a time. A larger disk cannot be placed upon a smaller disk.

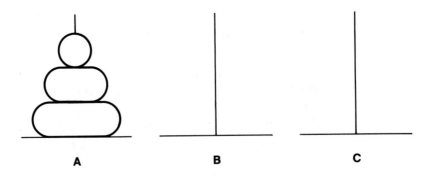

A   B   C

The first step is to move the top two disks out of the way so the largest disk can be moved to tower B:

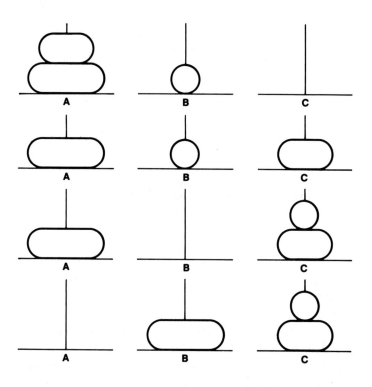

Once the largest disk is moved to tower B, move the smallest disk out of the way so the middle-sized disk can be placed on tower B:

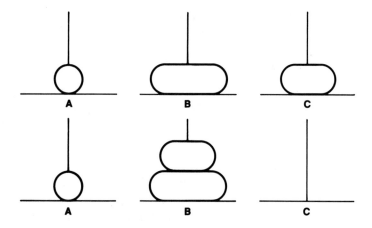

Last, place the smallest disk on tower B:

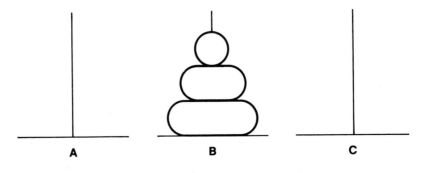

The routine **towers — of — hanoi ( )** is invoked with the following:

```
towers_of_hanoi (3, 'A', 'B', 'C');
```

Try invoking the routine with four disks and verify that it still moves the disks correctly. You will find that the number of moves increases with the number of disks.

The following routine counts the number of bits in a word that are 1. By performing a bitwise AND with a value contained in the word and the value −1, the least significant bit containing a 1 is inverted. If we count the number of ANDs required until the value equals zero, we will know the number of bits which contained the value 1. The following summarizes the code in the routine **bit — count( )**:

```
if (the value in word is not 0)
    return (1 + bit_count (result of bitwise AND))

else
    return (0)
```

If the value 7 is passed to the routine, the following processing is performed:

```
bit_count (7); or 0111
  return (1 + bitcount (7 & 7 - 1));

    bit_count (6); or 0110
      return (1 + bitcount (6 & 6 - 1));
```

```
bit_count (4); or 0100
       return (1 + bitcount (4 & 4 - 1));

             bit_count (0); or 0000
                return (0);

      1  -- result of bit_count(4)

      2  -- result of bit_count(6)

   3 -- result of bit_count(7)
```

The following routine places the ASCII representation of an integer value into a character string. For example, if the variable value contains 513, the following processing is performed by to—ascii( ):

```
to_ascii (value, string, 0);        /* original call */


to_ascii (513, string, 0)
   string[0] = value % 10 + '0';        the character '3'
   index++;
   value = value / 10;                  the value 51
   to_ascii (value, string, index);


   to_ascii (value, string, 1)
      string[1] = value % 10 + '0';        the character '1'
      index++;
      value = value / 10;                  the value 5
      to_ascii (value, string, index);


      to_ascii (value, string, 2)
         string[2] = value % 10 + '0';        the character '5'
         index++;
         value = value / 10;                  the value 0
                                        /* the ending condition   */
         string[3] = NULL;
         reverse (string,  0,  2);      /* puts the string in the */
                                        /* correct order "513"     */
```

Recursion is a very powerful tool when used properly, but there are trade-offs. Recursion can simplify difficult programming tasks, such as the Towers of Hanoi; however, it can be inefficient for routines that can be easily implemented with **for** or **while** loops because of the overhead of moving variables on and off the stack. The rule is not to use recursion if the process can be easily defined iteratively. This is true of some of the routines in this chapter, which can be implemented iteratively but have been presented to increase your understanding of recursive processes. You will examine additional recursive routines in Chapter 8.

```
/*
 * NAME: fact (value)
 *
 * FUNCTION: Returns the factorial of the value contained
 *           in the variable value, or -1 if the value is negative.
 *
 * EXAMPLE: x = fact (5); assigns x the value 120.
 *
 * VARIABLES USED: value: value to return the factorial of.
 *
 * PSEUDO CODE: if (the value is negative)
 *                  return (-1) -- error in negative value
 *
 *              if (the value is 1 or the value is 0 then)
 *                  return (1) -- by definition
 *
 *              else
 *                  return (value * fact (value - 1))
 *
 */

fact (value)
  int value;
  {
  if (value < 0)
    return (-1);  /* cannot take the factorial of a negative value */

  else if (value == 1 || value == 0)
    return (1);   /* by definition fact (1) and fact(0) are 1 */

  else
    return (value * fact (value - 1)); /* recursive call */
  }
```

```
/*
 * NAME: power (value, raised_to)
 *
 * FUNCTION: Returns the result of value raised to the power
 *           contained in the variable raised_to, or -1 if the
 *           value in raised_to is negative.
 *
 * EXAMPLE: x = power (5, 4); assigns x the value 625.
 *
 * VARIABLES USED: value: value to be raised to the power specified.
 *                 raised_to: power to raise the value to.
 *
```

```
* PSEUDO CODE: if (n is negative)
*                 return (-1)        -- won't raise a value to a
*                                       negative power
*
*              else if (n equals 0)   -- any value raised to the
*                 return (1)          -- value 0 is 1 by definition
*
*              else
*                 return (value * power (value, n - 1))
*
*/

float power (value, n)
  float value;
  int n;
 {
  if (n < 0)
   return (-1.0);        /* won't raise a value to a negative power */

  else if (n == 0)
   return (1.0);         /* any value raised to zero is one */
                         /* by definition                   */
  else
   return (value * power (value, n - 1));
 }
```

```
/*
 * NAME: print_rev (string)
 *
 * FUNCTION: Prints the contents of the character string
 *           in reverse order.
 *
 * EXAMPLE: if string contains "This is it"
 *          print_rev (string); prints "ti si sihT"
 *
 * VARIABLES USED: string: pointer to the character string.
 *
 * PSEUDO CODE: if (the letter in the *string is not NULL)
 *                 invoke print_rev with ++string (next letter)
 *                 print letter referenced by *(--string)
 *
 *              return
 *
 */

print_rev (string)
  char *string;
 {
  if (*string != NULL)
   {
    print_rev (++string);
    putchar(*(--string));
   }
 }
```

```
/* if the *string is not NULL, we will increment string and see
 * if the next value referenced by *string is NULL.  Once *string
 * points to NULL, we can begin working our way back by decrementing
 * string and printing the letter it points to.  Once we have
 * printed the letter which was originally the first letter in the
 * string, control is returned to the calling routine.
 */
```

```
/*
 * NAME: string_rev (string, start, end)
 *
 * FUNCTION: Reverses the characters in a string, or substring
 *           contained in the string.
 *
 * EXAMPLE: if string contains "THIS IS IT"
 *          string_rev (string, 5, 6); => THIS SI IT
 *          string_rev (string, 0, 9); => TI SI SIHT
 *          string_rev (string, 10, 11); => -1 is returned -- error
 *                                           in the starting location.
 *
 * VARIABLES USED: string: contains the string to reverse.
 *                 start: index to the first character to reverse.
 *                 end: index to the last character to reverse.
 *                 temp: temporary storage for the character swap.
 *
 * ROUTINES CALLED: string_length (); returns number of characters
 *                                     in the string.
 *
 * PSEUDO CODE: get the string length
 *              if (the starting location is > than the string length)
 *                return (-1) -- error in the starting location
 *
 *              if (the ending location is > than the string length)
 *                assign end to the location of the last
 *                character in the string
 *
 *              if (the starting location >= the ending location)
 *                return -- ending condition
 *
 *              else
 *               assign temp the value of string[start]
 *               assign string[start] the value in string[end]
 *               assign string[end] the value in temp
 *               string_rev (string, ++start, --end) -- recursive call
 *
 */
```

```
string_rev (string, start, end)
  char string[];
  int start, end;
{
  int length; /* length of the string */

  char temp;  /* temporary storage for the character swap */

  length = string_length (string);

  if (start >= length)
    return (-1);

  else if (end >= length)        /* assign end to the last character */
    end = length - 1;            /* in the string */

  if (start >= end)
    return;                      /* the string is reversed */

  else                           /* otherwise swap the letters and */
  {                              /* invoke string_rev() recursively */

    temp = string[start];

    string[start] = string[end];

    string[end] = temp;

    string_rev (string, ++start, --end); /* recursive call */

  }
}
```

```
/*
 * NAME: string_length (string)
 *
 * FUNCTION: Returns the number of characters contained the string.
 *
 * EXAMPLE: if string contains "this is it"
 *          x = string_length (string); assigns x the value 10.
 *
 * VARIABLES USED: string: pointer to the character string.
 *
 * PSEUDO CODE:  if (the letter referenced by string is NULL)
 *                   return (0) -- ending condition
 *
```

```
*                else
*                    return (1 + string_length (++string))
*
*/

string_length (string)
  char *string;
 {
  if (*string == NULL)  /* end of the string */
    return (0);

  else
    return (1 + string_length (++string));  /* recursive call */
 }
```

```
/*
 * NAME: towers_of_hanoi (n, x, y, z);
 *
 * FUNCTION: Performs the Towers of Hanoi algorithm to move
 *           the number of disk specified to the selected tower
 *           without allowing a smaller disk to be placed upon
 *           a larger disk.
 *
 * EXAMPLE: towers_of_hanoi (n, 'A', 'B', 'C');
 *
 * VARIABLES USED: n: contains the number of disk to move.
 *                 x, y, z: contains the character names of
 *                          each tower (A, B, C)
 *
 */

  towers_of_hanoi (n, x, y, z)
    int n;
    char x, y, z;
   {
    if (n < 1)
     printf ("No disk present on tower\n");

    else if (n == 1)
      printf ("Move top disk on tower %c to tower %c\n", x, y);

    else
     {
      towers_of_hanoi (n - 1, x, z, y);
      printf ("Move top disk on tower %c to tower %c\n", x, y);
      towers_of_hanoi (n - 1, z, y, x);
     }
   }
```

```
/*
 * NAME: bit_count (word)
 *
 * FUNCTION: Returns the number of bits in a word which are 1.
 *
 * EXAMPLE: x = bit_count (255); assigns x the value 8.
 *
 * VARIABLES USED: word: contains the bits to examine.
 *                 result: result of the bitwise AND of the
 *                         value in word and the value - 1.
 *
 * PSEUDO CODE: if (the value in word is not 0)
 *                 return (1 + bit_count (value & value - 1))
 *
 *              else
 *                 return (0)
 *
 *
 */
```

```
/* this routine utilizes the fact that a bitwise and of a value and
 * the value - 1 causes the least significant 1 bit to be eliminated.
 *
 *        1001 (9) & 1000 (9 - 1 = 8) produces 1000
 *
 * if this process is continued until the value equals zero, we only
 * need to count the number of iterations required to know the number
 * of bits which were originally one.  in this case the second iteration
 * causes the value to be 0, which is also the number of bits which
 * were originally one in the value 9.
 */

unsigned int bit_count (word)
  unsigned int word;
{
 if (word == 0)   /* stopping point for recursive calls */
    return (0);

  else
    return (1 + bit_count (word & (word - 1)));   /* recursive call */
}
```

```
/*
 * NAME: to_ascii (value, ascii_string, index);
 *
 * FUNCTION: Converts an integer value to its ASCII representation.
 *
 * EXAMPLES: to_ascii (255, string, 0); assigns string "255"
 *           to_ascii (-33, string, 0); assigns string "-33"
 *
```

```
*  VARIABLES USED: value: contains the integer value to convert to
*                        ASCII.
*                  string: contains the ASCII representation of the
*                          integer value.
*                  index: index into the character string.
*                  sign: contains the value to convert to ASCII.  if the
*                        value contained in sign is less than zero the
*                        sign of the value is negative.
*
*  ROUTINES CALLED: string_rev(): reverses the characters contained
*                                 in a string.
*
*  MACROS USED: abs_val(): returns the absolute value of an expression.
*
*  PSEUDO CODE: store the value in sign
*
*               store the ASCII representation of the least significant
*               digit into string[index] -- if value contains 126, the
*               value 6 will be stored
*
*               increment index in preparation of the next character
*
*               remove the least significant digit from value -- if value
*               contains 126, removing the least significant digit causes
*               value to contain 12
*
*               if (the new value is > 0)
*                  invoke to_ascii (new value, string, index)
*
*               else
*                  if (the sign of the value is negative)
*                     place the minus sign '-' in string[index]
*                     increment index in preparation of NULL
*
*               append NULL to the character string
*
*               reverse the contents of the character string -- if the
*               original value contained 126, the contents of the
*               character string is 621.  the routine string_rev()
*               will place the string in the correct order.
*
*/

to_ascii (value, string, index)
  int value;
  char string[];
  int index;

  {
    int sign = value;

    string[index++] = (abs_val(value) % 10) + '0';

    value /= 10;    /* removes the least significant digit */
```

```
  if (abs_val(value) > 0)
   to_ascii (value, string, index);

  else
   {
    if (sign < 0)
      string[index++] = '-';

    string[index] = NULL;

    string_rev (string, 0, index-1);
   }
}
```

C H A P T E R

Sorting Routines

Many programming applications require data to be processed in either ascending (lowest to highest) or descending (highest to lowest) order. In such instances, a *sorting algorithm* is used to place the data in order. This chapter will introduce three sorting algorithms: the bubble sort, Shell sort, and quick sort.

All of the routines in Chapter 7 were based on the type *array_ type*. Consequently, duplicate routines for arrays of different types do not need to be developed. If you write a routine that sorts an array in ascending order, and then you develop a second routine to sort an array in descending order, you have needlessly duplicated your programming efforts. To avoid having to duplicate routines, you pass the array and the number of elements in the array to the sorting routine and pass a pointer to a function that specifies the desired order of the elements (ascending or descending).

The routines **comp_ascending ( )** and **comp_descending ( )** are used in the sorting routines to specify whether or not the values contained in the arrays actually need to be exchanged. The first **comp—ascending (x,y)** will return **TRUE** if the value in **x** is greater than the value contained in **y**, or **FALSE** if the value in **x** is less than the value in **y**. Likewise, the routine **comp—descending (x,y)** will return **TRUE** if the value in **x** is less than the value in **y**, or **FALSE** if the value in **x** is greater than the value in **y**.

Bubble Sort

The bubble sort is one of the most popular sorting algorithms because of its simplicity. It is so named because with each iteration, the value moves, almost like a bubble, to the top of the array. Because it compares each adjacent element, however, the bubble sort is inefficient for large arrays. If the number of elements in your array exceeds 30, you should employ a sorting algorithm other than the bubble sort.

If the routine **comp—ascending (x,y)** is invoked by this code

```
bubble_sort (array, 5, comp_ascending);
```

and the array contains these values

0	44
1	33
2	55
3	22
4	11

then the first iteration of the bubble sort will perform four evaluations:

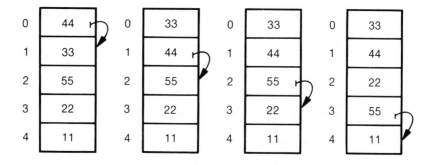

Since the largest value in the array (ascending order assumed) is in the correct location after the first iteration, you only need to examine the first four elements in the array during the second iteration of the sort. The second iteration will cause three evaluations to be performed:

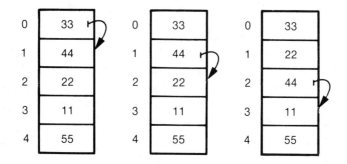

In the third pass, only two elements are exchanged:

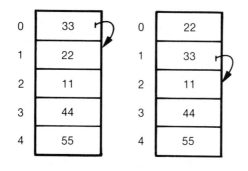

The final iteration ensures that the first two elements in the array are in the correct order and results in the final exchange:

Result

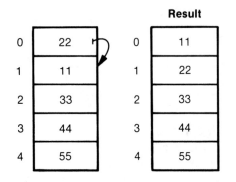

The routine uses the function pointer **out—of—sequence**, which deserves additional explanation.

```
int (*out_of_sequence)();
```

If you examine the contents of the first set of parentheses, you see that the variable **out—of—sequence** is a pointer. The other set of parentheses, ( ); specifies that **out—of—sequence** is a pointer to a function; **int** is the type of value returned by the function. If you tie all of this information together, **out—of—sequence** becomes *a pointer to a function that returns the type* **int**. If the first set of parentheses is removed, the variable becomes *a function returning a pointer to the type* **int**.

```
int *out_of_sequence ();
```

Shell Sort

The Shell sort was developed by Donald Shell to address the bubble sort's inefficiency with large arrays. The Shell sort differs from the bubble sort in that it first compares elements that are spaced farther apart and then adjacent elements, which tends to remove much of the array's disorder in the early iterations. The Shell sort uses a variable called **gap** that is initially set to the number of elements in the array divided by 2. The contents of **gap** specify the distance between the elements in the array that we will examine. For example, consider the following array:

0	1011
1	1088
2	1022
3	1077
4	1033
5	1066
6	1044
7	1055

$$gap = num\_elements / 2$$
$$= 8 / 2$$
$$= 4$$

In this example, the elements will initially be separated by a gap of 4. The first iteration of the array compares all of the elements separated by this distance. This process is repeated until no exchanges with a gap of 4 occur:

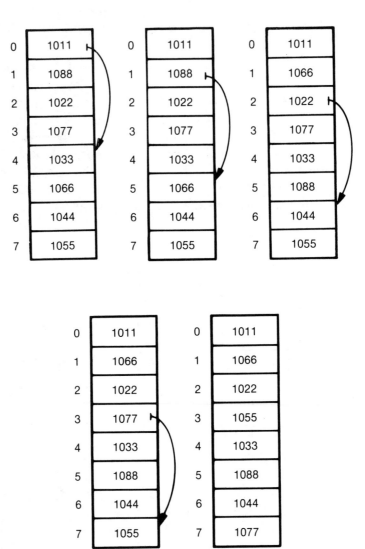

Once no exchanges with a gap of 4 occur, you reassign the value of **gap** to gap divided by 2 and repeat the process until no exchanges occur again.

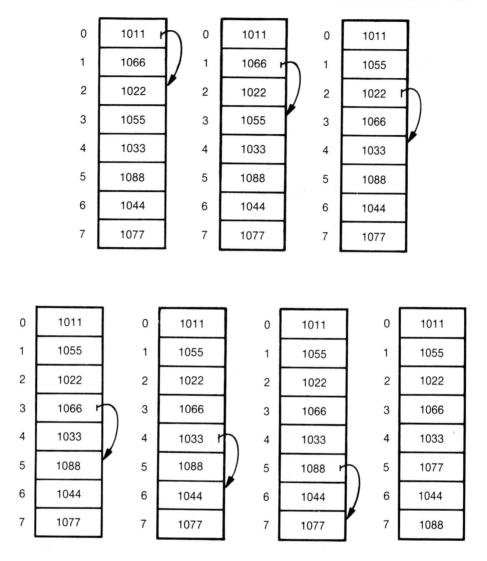

When no exchanges with a gap of 2 occur, you reassign the value of **gap** and start the process with **gap** equal to 1.

Since an exchange did occur, you iterate a second time and a third time.

After three iterations, no more exchanges occur and the array is sorted.

No exchanges

0	1011
1	1022
2	1033
3	1044
4	1055
5	1066
6	1077
7	1088

Quick Sort

Although the Shell sort increases the efficiency of your sort as the size of your array increases, it too has limitations. The quick sort, which is a recursive sorting algorithm, will increase the speed of your sort as the size of your array approaches 150 to 200 elements. In fact, the quick sort is one of the fastest array-sorting algorithms in use today. The quick sort sorts an array by breaking it down into a series of smaller sorted lists. For example, if the following array is passed to the routine

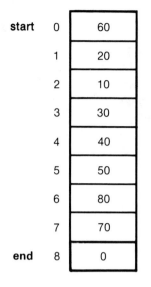

you will select the value referenced by **array[((start + end)/2)]**, or in this case, **array[4]**, to be your **list—separator**. Any values in the array that are less than or equal to the value contained within the **list—separator** will be placed into one list and the values that are greater will be placed into a second list.

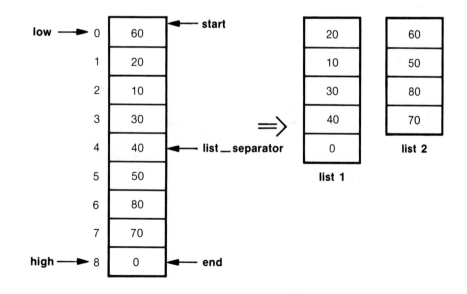

The same process is then carried out on each sublist until it contains only one element. At that point the array will be sorted.

Figure 8-1 describes the sequence in which the sublists are constructed. Fundamentally, the lists are split into two parts: the smaller items are in the left-hand list, and the larger items are in the right-hand list. This process is repeated until there is only one item in each list and the items are sorted from left to right.

If the following array is passed to the quick sort routine to be sorted in ascending order, it is first divided into two lists.

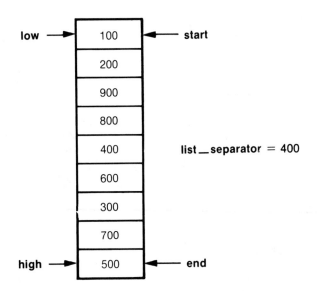

The variable **low** is assigned to the first element in the list. The variable **high** is assigned to the last element in the list. The variable **low** is incremented until **array[low]** contains a value that is greater than or equal to the **list—separator** (the value must be greater than or equal because this is an ascending-order sort).

```
while (array[low] < list_separator)
      low++;
```

Once **array[low]** contains a value that is greater than or equal to the value contained in **list—separator**, the while loop is terminated, and the value in **high** is decremented until **array[high]** contains a value that is less than or equal to the **list—separator**.

```
while (array[high] > list_separator)
       high--;
```

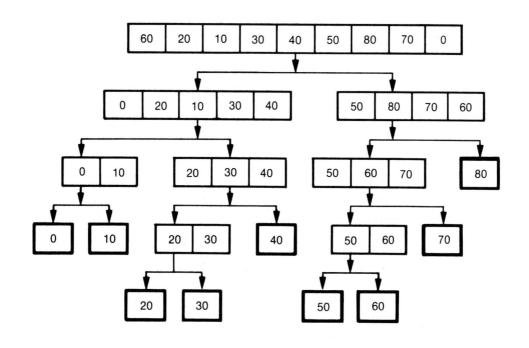

Figure 8-1. *Sequence of sublist construction using a quick sort*

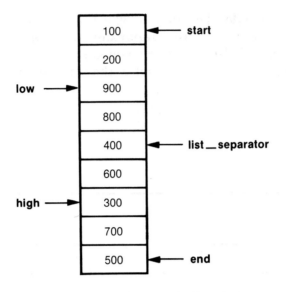

When the value contained in **array[high]** is less than or equal to the value contained in **list—separator**, the while loop terminates and the values contained in **low** and **high** are compared. If the value in **low** is less than the value contained in **high**, the values are exchanged.

```
while (array[low] < array[list_separator])
     low++;

while (array[high] > array [list_separator])
     high--;

if (low < high)
     exchange_values(&array[low], &array[high]);
```

The process is then repeated until **low** is greater than **high**.

```
do
{
    while (array[low] < list_separator)
         low++;

    while (array[high] > list_separator)
         high--;

    if (low < high)
         exchange_values(&array[low++], &array[high--]);
    else if (low == high)
         low++;

}
while (low <= high);
```

Once the value in **low** is greater than the value in **high**, you have your two lists. The first contains the elements from **start** to **high**, and the second contains the elements from **low** to **end**.

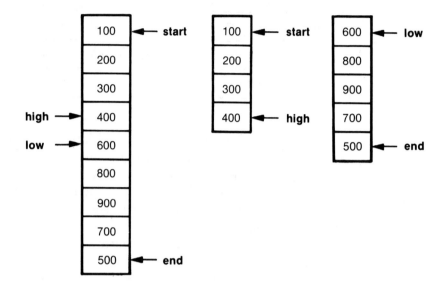

You will then pass each list to **quick_sort( )**, and they too are subdivided into lists. This process will continue until each list contains only one element.

If you invoke **quick_sort( )** by

```
quick_sort (array, 0, 4, comp_ascending);
```

the following processing is performed:

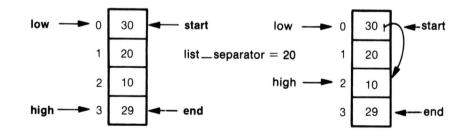

quick＿sort is then called twice with the following sublists:

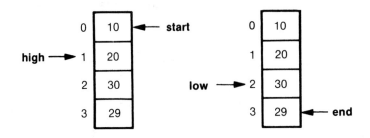

Selecting the proper sorting algorithm has a definite impact on the execution time of your routines. Most compilers that provide a sorting routine normally use the quick sort. If you place all three routines listed in this chapter into a file called **sort.c**, each of your routines can easily access the proper sorting algorithm. If you experiment with each routine and arrays of 30, 300, 3000, you should find that the execution time for each routine is almost equal for an array of size 30, the bubble sort is slower for an array of 300 elements, and the quick sort is much more efficient for an array of 3000 elements.

```
/*
 * NAME: comp_ascending (x, y)
 *
 * FUNCTION: Returns TRUE if the value contained in x is greater
 *           than the value contained in y, otherwise FALSE is
 *           returned.
 *
 * EXAMPLES: if (comp_ascending (5, 4))  -- returns TRUE
 *           if (comp_ascending (5, 5))  -- returns FALSE
 *
 * VARIABLES USED: x, y: values to compare.
 *
 * PSEUDO CODE: if (the value in x is greater than the value in y)
 *                 return (1) -- the Boolean TRUE
 *
 *              else
 *                 return (0) -- the Boolean FALSE
 *
 */

comp_ascending (x, y)
  array_type x, y;
  {

  return ((x > y) ? TRUE : FALSE);

  }
```

```
/*
 * NAME: comp_descending (x, y)
 *
 * FUNCTION: Returns TRUE if the value contained in x is less
 *           than the value contained in y, otherwise FALSE is
 *           returned.
 *
 * EXAMPLES: if (comp_descending (2, 4))  -- returns TRUE
 *           if (comp_descending (5, 5))  -- returns FALSE
 *
 * VARIABLES USED: x, y: values to compare.
 *
 * PSEUDO CODE: if (the value in x is less than the value in y)
 *                 return (1) -- the Boolean TRUE
 *
 *              else
 *                 return (0) -- the Boolean FALSE
 *
 */

comp_descending (x, y)
  array_type x, y;
 {

  return ((x < y) ? TRUE : FALSE);

 }
```

```
/*
 * NAME: exchange_values (x, y)
 *
 * FUNCTION: Exchanges the values contained in the variables
 *           x and y.
 *
 * EXAMPLE: exchange_values (&array[i], &array[j]);
 *
 * VARIABLES USED: x, y: pointers to the values to exchange.
 *                 temp: temporary storage for the exchange.
 *
 * PSEUDO CODE: assign temp the value contained in the location
 *                 referenced by x
 *              assign the value referenced by y to the
 *                 location referenced by x
 *              assign temp to the value contained in the location
 *                 referenced by y
 *
 */

exchange_values (x, y)
  array_type *x, *y;
 {
  array_type temp;
```

```
/* we have to use pointers to the variables if we want to modify
 * the values they contain.
 */

  temp = *x;     /* save the value referenced by x */

  *x = *y;       /* assign the variable referenced by x the
                    value referenced by y */

  *y = temp;     /* assign the variable referenced by y the value
                    that was originally referenced by x */
}
```

```
/*
 * NAME: bubble_sort (array, num_elements, out_of_sequence)
 *
 * FUNCTION: Sorts the contents of an array in the order specified
 *           by out_of_sequence (ascending or descending).  The
 *           pointer to the function specifying the order to sort
 *           the contents of the array in is named out_of_sequence
 *           to increase the readability of the routine as follows:
 *
 *           if ((*out_of_sequence) (array[i], array[i+1]))
 *             exchange_values (&array[i], &array[i+1]);
 *
 * VARIABLES USED: array: the array of values to sort.
 *                 num_elements: number of elements in the array.
 *                 out_of_sequence: pointer to the function which
 *                                  specifies the sorting sequence.
 *
 * ROUTINES CALLED: comp_ascending (x, y); returns TRUE if the value in
 *                                  x is greater than the value
 *                                  in y.
 *                  comp_descending (x, y); returns TRUE if the value
 *                                  in x is less than the
 *                                  value in y.
 *                  exchange_values (x, y); exchanges the values in
 *                                  the variables x and y.
 *
 * PSEUDO CODE: initialize j to the number of elements in the array
 *
 *              while (the value in j is greater than 1)
 *                assign i the value  0
 *
 *                while (the value in i is less than the value in j)
 *                  if (array[i] and array[i+1] are out of order)
 *                    swap the values in array[i] and array[i+1]
 *
 *                  increment i
 *
 *                decrement j
 *
```

```
*           return -- the array is sorted
*
*/

bubble_sort (array, num_elements, out_of_sequence)
  array_type array[];            /* values to sort */
  int num_elements;              /* number of values */
  int (*out_of_sequence) ();     /* specifies the sorting order */
{
  int i, j;

  j = num_elements;

  while (j-- > 1)
    for (i = 0; i < j; i++)
      if ((*out_of_sequence) (array[i], array[i+1]))
        exchange_values (&array[i], &array[i+1]);
}
```

```
/*
 * NAME: shell_sort (array, num_elements, out_of_sequence)
 *
 * FUNCTION: Sort the contents of the array in the order
 *           specified by the function referenced by
 *           the function pointer out_of_sequence.
 *
 *           The function pointer is named out_of_sequence to
 *           increase the readability of the routine as illustrated
 *           below:
 *
 *           if ((*out_of_sequence) (array[i], array[i + gap]))
 *             exchange_values (&array[i], &array[i + gap]);
 *
 * VARIABLES USED: array: the array of values to sort.
 *                 num_elements: number of values in the array.
 *                 out_of_sequence: pointer to the function which
 *                                  specifies the order of the
 *                                  sort (ascending or descending).
 *                 i: index into the array.
 *                 gap: the distance between the elements to examine.
 *                 exchge_occurred: TRUE if an exchange occurred.
 *                                  FALSE if no exchange occurred.
 *
 * ROUTINES CALLED: comp_ascending (x, y); returns TRUE if x is > y
 *                                    or FALSE if x <= y.
 *                  comp_descending (x, y); returns TRUE  if x < y
 *                                    or FALSE if x >= y.
 *                  exchange_values (&x, &y); exchanges the values
 *                                    contained in the
 *                                    variables x and y.
 *
 * PSEUDO CODE: initialize gap = (the number of elements / 2)
 *
```

```
*                   while (the value in gap is > 0)
*                       set exchge_occurred to FALSE
*                       while (an exchange occurred with the current gap)
*                           set i = 0
*                           while (i is less than num_elements - gap)
*
*                           if (array[i] and array[i + gap] are out of order)
*                               exchange the values in array[i] and array[i + gap]
*                               set exchge_occurred to TRUE
*
*                           increment i
*
*                       assign gap = gap / 2
*
*                   return -- the array is sorted
*
*/
shell_sort (array, num_elements, out_of_sequence)
  array_type array[];
  int num_elements;
  int (*out_of_sequence) (); /* pointer to the function specifying
                                the sorting order */
  {
  int i;

  int exchge_occurred;   /* FALSE if no exchange was made */

  int gap = num_elements / 2;

  do

      do
        {
          exchge_occurred = FALSE;
          for (i = 0; i < num_elements - gap; i++)
            if ((*out_of_sequence) (array[i], array[i + gap]))
              {
                exchange_values (&array[i], &array[i + gap]);

                exchge_occurred = TRUE;
              }
        }
      while (exchge_occurred);

  while ((gap /= 2) > 0);
  }
```

```
/*
 * NAME: shell_rec (array, num_elements, out_of_sequence, gap)
 *
 * FUNCTION: Recursively sort the contents of the array in
 *           the order specified by the function referenced
 *           by the function pointer out_of_sequence.
 *
```

```
*               The function pointer is named out_of_sequence to
*               increase the readability of the routine as illustrated
*               below:
*
*               if ((*out_of_sequence) (array[i], array[i + gap]))
*                 exchange_values (&array[i], &array[i + gap]);
*
* VARIABLES USED: array: the array of values to sort.
*                 num_elements: number of values in the array.
*                 out_of_sequence: pointer to the function which
*                                  specifies the order of the
*                                  sort (ascending or descending).
*                 i: index into the array.
*                 gap: the distance between the elements to examine.
*                 exchge_occurred: TRUE if an exchange occurred with
*                                  the current gap otherwise FALSE if
*                                  no exchange occurred.
*
* ROUTINES CALLED: comp_ascending (x, y); returns TRUE if x is > y
*                                          or FALSE if x < y.
*                  comp_descending (x, y); returns TRUE if x < y
*                                          or FALSE if x > y.
*                  exchange_values (&x, &y); exchanges the values
*                                           contained in x and y.
*
* PSEUDO CODE: initiize exchge_occurred to FALSE
*              while (an exchange occurred with the current gap)
*                set i = 0
*                if (array[i] and array[i + gap] are out of order)
*                  exchange the values in array[i] and array[i + gap]
*                  set exchge_occurred to TRUE
*
*                increment i
*
*                if (gap / 2 is greater than 0)
*                  invoke shell sort with gap/2 -- recursive call
*
*                return -- the array is sorted
*
*/

shell_rec (array, num_elements, out_of_sequence, gap)
  array_type array[];
  int num_elements;
  int (*out_of_sequence) (); /* pointer to the function specifying
                                the sorting order */
  int gap;    /* distance between the elements to examine */
{
  int i;

  int exchge_occurred;  /* FALSE if no exchange was made */

  do
    {
      exchge_occurred = FALSE;
      for (i = 0; i < num_elements - gap; i++)
        if ((*out_of_sequence) (array[i], array[i + gap]))
          {
```

```
            exchange_values (&array[i], &array[i + gap]);

            exchge_occurred = TRUE;
         }
      }
   while (exchge_occurred);

   if  ((gap /= 2) > 0)
      shell_rec (array, num_elements, out_of_sequence, gap);
}
```

```
/*
 * NAME: quick_sort (array, start, end, put_in_list)
 *
 * FUNCTION: Sorts the elements in the array based upon the
 *           order specified in the function pointer
 *           put_in_list.  The pointer to the function
 *           is given the name put_in_list to increase
 *           the readability of the routine as follows:
 *
 *           while ((*put_in_list) (array[low], list_separator))
 *             low++;
 *
 *           Since the routines which compare the values return
 *           TRUE when the values should be exchanged, the value
 *           TRUE tells us to put array[low] in the list.
 *
 * EXAMPLE: quick_sort (array, 0, 10, comp_ascending);
 *
 * VARIABLES USED: array: the array of values to sort.
 *                 start: first element in the array (list).
 *                 end: last element in the array (list).
 *                 put_in_list: pointer to the function
 *                              which specifies the sorting order
 *                              (ascending or descending) of the
 *                              elements contained in the array.
 *                 low, high: indices into the array.
 *                 list_separator: All values in the array which are
 *                                 <= to list_separator are placed
 *                                 in one list and the array values
 *                                 which are greater are put in a
 *                                 second list.
 *
 * ROUTINES CALLED: comp_ascending (x, y); returns TRUE if x > y or
 *                                          FALSE if x < y.
 *
 *                  comp_descending (x, y); returns TRUE if x < y or
 *                                          FALSE if x > y.
 *
 *                  exchange_values (x, y); exchanges the values contained
 *                                          in the variables x and y.
 *
```

```
* PSEUDO CODE: initialize low to the value in start
*              initialize high to the value in end
*              initialize list_separator to the value (end + start) / 2
*
*              while (low <= high)
*                 while (array [low] is < than the list separator)
*                    increment low to point to the next value
*
*                 while (array [high] is > than the list separator)
*                    decrement high to point to the next value
*
*                 if (low < high)
*                    exchange the values in array[low] and array[high]
*                    increment low
*                    decrement high
*                 else if (low is equal to high)
*                    increment low
*
*              if (a lower list exist)
*                 invoke quick_sort with the lower list
*
*              if (a higher list exist)
*                 invoke quick_sort with the higher list
*
*/
quick_sort (array, start, end, put_in_list)
  array_type array[];
  int start;                      /* first value in list */
  int end;                        /* last value in list */
  int (*put_in_list)();   /* pointer to the function which */
                          /* specifies the sorting order */
{
  int low = start;
  int high = end;

  int list_separator = array [(start + end) / 2];

  /* break list into two sublist */

  do {

    while ((*put_in_list) (list_separator, array[low]))
      low++;

    while ((*put_in_list) (array[high], list_separator))
      high--;

    if (low < high)
      exchange_values (&array[low++], &array[high--]);
    else if (low == high)
      low++;

  }
  while (low <= high);

  /* invoke quick sort with both list */
```

```
  if (start < high)
    quick_sort (array, start, high, put_in_list);

  if (low < end)
    quick_sort (array, low, end, put_in_list);
}
```

C H A P T E R

Trigonometric Functions and Character Conversion

The routines in this chapter provide trigonometric functions and character-conversion capability. Since C was developed as a systems programming language, the trigonometric functions are not included with most C compilers. The following trigonometric routines are based upon a Taylor series approximation of the sine function. This chapter will not address the approximation algorithm itself because its math is beyond the scope of this text.

Routines that provide approximations to roots (square, cube, and so on) via the Newton Raphson root approximation algorithm are also included. Most compilers providing this capability use the Newton Raphson approximation. In addition, the chapter includes a prime number routine and a routine to develop an ASCII Hex/Octal/ Decimal chart similar to that in Appendix A. At the end of the chapter is a series of routines to convert from decimal to octal, decimal to hexadecimal, decimal to binary, and back again.

```
/*
 * NAME: sin (radians)
 *
 * FUNCTION: Returns the sine of the angle in the variable radians.
 *
 * EXAMPLE: x = sin (PI/2); assigns x the value 1.
 *
 * VARIABLES USED: radians: the angle to approximate the sine of.
 *                 approx: approximation of the sine of the angle.
 *                 difference: the amount the approximation changed
 *                             in the last iteration.
 *                 inc: count of the iterations.
 *
 * MACROS USED: abs_val(); returns the absolute value of a value.
 *              square();  returns the square of a value.
 *
 * PSEUDO CODE: Perform a Taylor Series approximation of the sine.
 *
 */

double sin (radians)
  double radians;
  {
  double approx = (double) radians;      /* initial approximation
                                            of the sine of the angle */

  double difference = (double) radians;

  int inc = 1;                           /* count of the iterations */

  do
    {
    difference = (difference * -square(radians))/
            ((2.0 * inc) * (2.0 * inc + 1.0));

    approx = approx + difference;

    inc++;
    }
  while (abs_val(difference) >= 0.00001);

  return (approx);                       /* in radians */
  }
```

```
/*
 * NAME: cos (radians)
 *
 * FUNCTION: Returns the cosine of angle contained in the variable
 *           radians.
 *
 * EXAMPLE: x = cos (y);
 *
 * VARIABLES USED: radians: the angle (in radians) to approximate
 *                          the cosine of.
 *
 * ROUTINES CALLED: sin (); returns the sine of an angle.
 *
 * PSEUDO CODE: compute the cosine of the angle via the expression
 *                 cos = (sin(PI/2 - radians))
 *
 *              return (the cosine of the angle)
 *
 */

double cos (radians)
  double radians;
 {
  double sin ();

  return (sin (PI / 2.0 - radians));
 }
```

```
/*
 * NAME: tan (radians)
 *
 * FUNCTION: Returns the tangent of the angle contained in the
 *           variable radians.
 *
 * EXAMPLE: x = tan (y);
 *
 * VARIABLES USED: radians: the angle (in radians) to approximate
 *                          the tangent of.
 *
 * MACROS USED: abs_val(); returns the absolute value of a value.
 *
 * ROUTINES CALLED: sin (); returns the sine of an angle.
 *                  cos (); returns the cosine of an angle.
 *
 * PSEUDO CODE: get the cosine of the angle
 *              if (the cosine is zero)
 *                 return (UNDEFINED) -- can't divide by zero
 *
 *              else
 *                 compute the tangent via the expression
 *                   tan = (sin(radians) / cos(radians))
 *
 *              return (the tangent of the angle)
 */
```

```
double tan (radians)
  double radians;
 {
  double sin (), cos ();
  double cosine;

  cosine = cos (radians);            /* the cosine of the angle */

  if (abs_val(cosine) <= 0.0001)  /* can't divide by zero */
    return (UNDEFINED);

  else
    return (sin (radians) / cosine);
 }
```

```
/*
 * NAME: cotan (radians)
 *
 * FUNCTION: Returns the cotangent of angle contained in the variable
 *           radians.
 *
 * EXAMPLE: x = cotan (y);
 *
 * VARIABLES USED: radians: the angle (in radians) to approximate
 *                          the cotangent of.
 *
 * MACROS USED: abs_val(); returns the absolute value of a value.
 *
 * ROUTINES CALLED: sin (); returns the sine of an angle.
 *                  cos (); returns the cosine of an angle.
 *
 * PSEUDO CODE: get the sine of the angle
 *              if (the sine is zero)
 *                 return (UNDEFINED) --  can't divide by zero
 *
 *              else
 *                 compute the cotangent via the expression
 *                    cotan = (cos (radians) / sin (radians))
 *
 *              return (the cotangent of the angle)
 */
double cotan (radians)
  double radians;
 {
  double sine;                       /* the sine of the angle */
  double sin(), cos();

  sine = sin (radians);

  if (abs_val(sine) <= 0.0001)  /* can't divide by zero */
    return (UNDEFINED);

  else
    return (cos (radians) / sine);
 }
```

```
/*
 * NAME: arctan (radians);
 * FUNCTION: Returns the arctangent of the value contained in radians.
 * EXAMPLE: x = arctan (angle);
 */
double arctan (radians)
  double radians;
{
  static double argument_table [10] = { 0117188, 0.023438, 0.046875,
      0.093750, 0.187500, 0.3750, 0.750,1.500, 3.000, 6.00 };
  static double arctan_table [10] = { 0117182, 0.0234332, 0.0468407,
      0.093476781, 0.185347950, 0.358770670, 0.643501109, 0.982793723,
      1.249045772, 1.405647649 };
  double c0 = 1.0000000, c3 = -0.3333333, c5 =  0.2000000, c7 = -0.1428571;
  double half_pi = (3.1415927 / 2.0);
  double max_value = 32.0 / 3.0;
  double estimated_arctan;                /* value returned */
  double angle_squared;                   /* radians * radians */
  int table_index;
  int negative_value;                     /* TRUE if angle is negative */
  int large_value;                        /* TRUE if angle is > 32 / 3 */
  if (radians < 0.0)                      /* is the angle negative? */
    {
      negative_value = TRUE;
      radians = abs_val(radians);
    }
  else
    negative_value = FALSE;
  if (radians > max_value)
    {
      large_value = TRUE;
      radians = 1.0 / radians;            /* invert the angle */
    }
  else
    large_value = FALSE;
  angle_squared = square(radians);
  if ((radians - argument_table [1]) < 0.0)
    if (large_value)
      estimated_arctan = half_pi - radians * (c0 + angle_squared *
                          (c3 + angle_squared * (c5 + angle_squared * c7)));
    else
      estimated_arctan = radians + radians * angle_squared *
                          (c3 + angle_squared * (c5 + angle_squared * c7));
  else
    {
      estimated_arctan = 0.0;
      for (table_index = 9; table_index >= 1; table_index--)
        if ((radians - argument_table[table_index]) > 0.0)
          {
            estimated_arctan += arctan_table [table_index];
            radians = (radians - argument_table [table_index]) /
                      (1.0 + radians * argument_table [table_index]);
          }
      angle_squared = square(radians);
      estimated_arctan += radians * (c0 + angle_squared *
                          (c3 + angle_squared * (c5 + angle_squared * c7)));
    }
    return ((negative_value) ? -estimated_arctan: estimated_arctan);
  }
```

```
/*
 * NAME: csc (radians)
 *
 * FUNCTION: Returns the cosecant of the angle contained in the
 *           variable radians.
 *
 * EXAMPLE: x = csc (y);
 *
 * VARIABLES USED: radians: the angle (in radians) to approximate
 *                          the cosecant of.
 *
 * MACROS USED: abs_val(); returns the absolute value of a value.
 *
 * ROUTINES CALLED: sin (); returns the sine of an angle.
 *
 * PSEUDO CODE: get the sine of the angle
 *              if (the sine is zero)
 *                  return (UNDEFINED) -- can't divide by zero
 *
 *              else
 *                compute the cosecant via the expression
 *                    csc = (1.0 / sin (radians))
 *
 *              return (the cosecant of the angle)
 */
double csc (radians)
  double radians;
 {
  double sine;
  double sin();

  sine = sin (radians);          /* sine of the angle */

  if (abs_val(sine) <= 0.0001)
    return (UNDEFINED);          /* can't divide by zero */

  else
    return (1.0 /sine);
 }
```

```
/*
 * NAME: sec (radians)
 *
 * FUNCTION: Returns the secant of the angle contained in the
 *           variable radians.
 *
 * EXAMPLE: x = sec (y);
 *
 * VARIABLES USED: radians: the angle (in radians) to approximate
 *                          the secant of.
 *
 * MACROS USED: abs_val(); returns the absolute value of a value.
 *
 * ROUTINES CALLED: cos (); returns the cosine of an angle.
 *
 * PSEUDO CODE: get the cosine of the angle
 *              if the (cosine is zero)
```

```
 *                 return (UNDEFINED) -- can't divide by zero
 *
 *              else
 *                 compute the secant via the expression
 *                    sec = (1.0 / cos (radians))
 *
 *              return (the secant of the value)
 */

double sec (radians)
  double radians;
{
  double cosine;                   /* the cosine of the angle */
  double cos();

  cosine = cos (radians);

  if (abs_val(cosine) <= 0.0001) /* can't divide by zero */
     return (UNDEFINED);

  else
     return (1.0 / cosine);
}
```

```
/*
 * NAME: is_prime (x)
 *
 * FUNCTION: Returns TRUE if the value contained in x is a prime
 *           number (a number only divisable by one and itself), or
 *           a FALSE if the value is not prime.
 *
 * EXAMPLE: if (is_prime (5)) returns TRUE.
 *
 * VARIABLES USED: x: the value to examine for prime.
 *                 divisor: the value the number is divided by.
 *                 prime: contains TRUE if the number is prime,
 *                        otherwise FALSE.
 *                 limit: when checking if a value is prime you
 *                        only need to examine to the square root
 *                        of the value.  limit contains the square
 *                        root of the value.
 *
 * PSEUDO CODE: if (the value is less than or equal to 0)
 *                 return (-1) -- won't take square root of
 *                                  0 or a negative value
 *
 *              initialize limit to the square root of the value
 *              initialize prime to TRUE
 *              initialize divisor to 2
 *              while (divisor <= limit and prime is TRUE)
 *                 if (value mod divisor is 0)
 *                    assign prime the value FALSE
 *                 increment divisor
 *
 *              return the value in prime (TRUE or FALSE)
 *
 */
```

```
is_prime (n)
  int n;            /* the value to examine */
{
  int divisor;
  int prime = TRUE;

  int limit;       /* contains the square root of n */

  float sqrt ();   /* returns the square root of a value */

  limit = sqrt (n * 1.0);  /* 1.0 converts the value to
                              the type float */

  for  (divisor = 2; divisor <= limit; divisor++)
    if (n % divisor == 0)
      {
       prime = FALSE;
       break;
      }
  return (prime);    /* TRUE or FALSE */
}
```

```
/*
 * NAME: sqrt (value)
 *
 * FUNCTION: Returns the square root of the value contained in
 *           in the variable value, or a -1 if the value is negative.
 *
 * EXAMPLE: x = sqrt (25); assigns x the value 5.
 *
 * VARIABLES USED: value: the value to approximate the
 *                        square root of.
 *                 x: approximation of the square root.
 *                 dx: result of the approximation of the root
 *                     in the first derivitive of the function.
 *                 min_tolerance: how close the approximation must be
 *                                to the actual solution.
 *                 difference: difference between the approximation
 *                             and the actual solution.
 *                 i: counter.
 *
 * MACROS USED: abs_val(); returns the absolute value of a value.
 *
 * PSEUDO CODE: initially approximate root to (value / 10)
 *
 *              if (the value is negative)
 *                 return (-1) -- can't take the square root of
 *                               a negative value
 *
 *              else
 *                 perform (the Newton Raphson root approximation)
 *
 */
```

```
float sqrt (value)
  float value;
{
  float x = value/10;  /* the approximation of the root */

  float dx;             /* the value of the approximation of the */
                        /* root in the first derivitive of the */
                        /* root function */

  double difference;    /* how close is the approximation to */
                        /* to the correct solution */

  double min_tolerance =  0.00001; /* how close the approximation */
                                   /* must be to the actual solution */
                                   /* before we stop  */

  int i;                /* count of the iterations performed */

  if (value < 0)
    return (-1.0);
  else if (value == 0) /* square root of zero is zero */
    return (0.0);

  for (i = 1; i < 20; i++)
   {
    dx = (value - square (x)) / (2.0 * x);

    x = x + dx;

    difference = value - square (x);  /* how close is the */
                                      /* approximation to */
                                      /* the actual solution */

    if (abs_val(difference) <= min_tolerance)
      break;                                   /* close enough */

   }
  return (x);  /* the approximation of the root */
}
```

```
/*
 * NAME: cube_root (value)
 *
 * FUNCTION: Returns the cube root of the value contained in
 *           in the variable value.
 *
 * EXAMPLE: x = cube_root (27); assigns x the value 3.
 *
 * VARIABLES USED: value: the value to approximate the
 *                        cube root of.
 *                 x: approximation of the cube root.
 *                 dx: result of the approximation of the root
 *                     in the first derivitive of the function.
```

```
 *                      min_tolerance: how close the approximation must
 *                                     be to the actual solution before
 *                                     we stop.
 *                      difference: difference between the approximation
 *                                  and the actual value.
 *                      i: counter.
 *
 * MACROS USED: abs_val(); returns the absolute value of a value.
 *
 * PSEUDO CODE: initially approximate the root to (value / 10)
 *
 *              perform (the Newton Raphson root approximation)
 *
 */

float cube_root (value)
  float value;
  {
  float x = value/10;    /* the approximation of the root */

  float dx;              /* the value of the approximation of the */
                         /* root in the first derivitive of the */
                         /* root function */

  double difference;     /* how close is the approximation to  */
                         /* to the actual solution */

  double min_tolerance =  0.00001; /* how close the approximation */
                                   /* must be to the actual solution */
                                   /* before we stop  */

  int i;                 /* count of the iterations performed */

  if (value == 0)
    return (0.0);        /* cube root of zero is zero */

  for (i = 1; i < 20; i++)
    {
    dx = (value - cube (x)) / (3.0 * square(x));
    x = x + dx;

    difference = value - cube(x); /* how close is the approximation */
                                  /* to the actual solution */

    if (abs_val(difference) <= min_tolerance)
      break;                                    /* close enough */
    }

  return (x);  /* the approximation of the root */
  }
```

```
/*
 * NAME: get_root (value, root)
 *
 * FUNCTION: Returns the root specified in the variable root
 *           of the value contained in the variable value.
 *
```

```
* EXAMPLE: x = get_root (27, 3); takes the cube root of 27 and
*                                assigns x the value 3.
*
* VARIABLES USED: value: the value to approximate the root of.
*                 root: value containing the root to take.
*                 x: approximation of the root.
*                 dx: result of the approximation of the root
*                     in the first derivitive of the function.
*                 min_tolerance: how close the approximation must
*                                be to the actual solution before
*                                we stop.
*                 difference: difference between the approximation
*                             and the actual solution.
*                 i: counter.
*
* MACROS USED: abs_val(); returns the absolute value of a power.
*              is_even(); returns 1 if the value is even
*                         or 0 if the value is odd.
*
* ROUTINES CALLED: power(); raises a value to an integer power.
*
* PSEUDO CODE: initially approximate the root to (value / 10)
*
*              if (the value is negative and the root is even)
*                 return (-1) -- can't take an even root of a
*                               negative value
*
*              else
*                 perform (the Newton Raphson root approximation)
*
*/

float get_root (value, root)
  float value;
  int root;
{
  float power();

  float x = value/10;   /* the approximation of the root */

  float dx;             /* the value of the approximation of the */
                        /* root in the first derivitive of the */
                        /* root function */

  double difference;    /* how close is the approximation */
                        /* to the correct solution. */

  double min_tolerance = 0.00001;  /* how close the approximation */
                                   /* must be to the actual */
                                   /* solution before we stop */

  int i;                /* count of the iterations performed */

  if (value < 0 && is_even(root)) /* can't take even root of */
    return (-1.0);                /* a negative number */

  else if (value == 0)
    return (0.0);                        /* root of zero is zero */
```

```
  for (i = 1; i < 100; i++)
    {
    dx = (value - power (x, root)) /
         (root * power(x, root - 1));

    x = x + dx;

    difference = value - power(x, root);   /* how close is the
                                              approximation to
                                              the actual solution */

    if (abs_val(difference) <= min_tolerance)
      break;                                /* close enough */
    }

  return (x);  /* the approximation of the root */
}
```

```
/* declared as external */

char *ascii [33] =      {"NUL", "SOH", "EXT", "EOT", "ENQ",
                         "ACK", "BEL", "BS ", "HT ", "HT ",
                         "LF ", "VT ", "FF ", "CR ", "SO ",
                         "SI* ", "DLE", "DC1", "DC2", "DC3",
                         "DC4", "NAK", "SYN", "ETB", "CAN",
                         "EM ", "SUB", "ESC", "FS ", "GS ",
                         "RS ", "US ", "BLANK"};

/*
 * NAME: ascii_chart (fp)
 *
 * FUNCTION:  Writes an ASCII HEX OCTAL DECIMAL chart to the file
 *            specified by fp.  If the user wants to display the
 *            chart to the screen the routine should be invoked
 *            with stdout.
 *
 * EXAMPLE: ascii_chart (stdout);
 *
 * VARIABLES USED: fp: pointer to the output file.
 *                 count: counter.
 *                 hex: string containing the hexadecimal equivalent
 *                      to count.
 *                 octal: string containing the octal equivalent
 *                        to count.
 *                 ascii: array of pointers to the ASCII characters
 *                        from 1 - 33.
 *
 * MACROS USED: is_printable_ascii(); returns TRUE if the value is a
 *                                    printable ASCII character,
 *                                    otherwise FALSE is returned.
 *
 * ROUTINES CALLED: to_octal_string(); converts a decimal value to octal
 *                                     and places the result in a string.
```

```
*                    to_hexadecimal_string(); converts a decimal value
*                                              to hexadecimal and places
*                                              the result in a string.
*
* PSEUDO CODE: for (count = 0 to 127)
*                  convert count to the octal string
*                  convert count to the hexadecimal string
*                  if (the value in count is a printable ASCII character)
*                      print the value
*
*                  else
*                      print the ASCII string contained in *ascii[count]
*
*                  print count and the octal, and hexadecimal strings
*
*                  return
*
*/

ascii_chart (fp)
  FILE *fp;
 {
  int count;
  extern char *ascii[];
  char hex[4];
  char octal[10];

  printf ("\tDECIMAL\t\tHEX\t\tOCTAL\t\tASCII\n");

  for (count = 0; count < 127; count++)
   {
     to_octal_string (count, octal);

     to_hexadecimal_string (count, hex);

     if (is_printable_ascii(count))
         fprintf (fp, "\t  %d\t\t %s\t\t %s\t\t %c\n", count, hex,
                  octal, count);
     else
         fprintf (fp, "\t  %d\t\t %s\t\t %s\t\t %s\n", count, hex,
                  octal, ascii[count]);
   }
 }
```

```
/*
 * NAME: hex_string_to_decimal (hex, decimal)
 *
 * FUNCTION: Converts a string containing an ASCII representation
 *           of a hexadecimal number to the corresponding decimal
 *           value.
 *
 * EXAMPLE: val = hex_string_to_decimal ("FF", &decimal);
 *
```

```
* VARIABLES USED: hex: pointer to the character string containing
*                      the ASCII representation of the  hexadecimal
*                      value.
*                 decimal: decimal equivalent.
*
* MACROS USED: to_uppercase(); converts a letter to UPPERCASE
*              is_hexadecimal(); returns TRUE if letter is an
*                      ASCII representation of a
*                      hexadecimal number, otherwise
*                      FALSE is returned.
*              to_decimal(); converts an ASCII digit '0' - '9'
*                      to its decimal value.
*
* PSEUDO CODE: initialize decimal value to 0
*
*              while (*hex is not NULL)
*                 convert *hex to UPPERCASE
*                 if (*hex is hexadecimal)
*                    convert it to decimal
*                    add the converted value to the
*                      decimal equivalent
*                    increment hex to point to the next
*                      character in the string
*                 else
*                    return (-1)   /* invalid character */
*
*              return (NO_ERROR)
*
*/


hex_string_to_decimal (hex, decimal)
  char *hex;
  int *decimal;  /* decimal equivalent */
{
  *decimal = 0;

  /* as long as the character in *hex is a valid hexadecimal
     value, convert it to decimal, otherwise return -1 */

  while (*hex)
    {
      *hex = to_uppercase(*hex);  /* convert each character to
                                     UPPERCASE to insure the
                                     characters a - f are valid */

    if (is_hexadecimal(*hex))
        {
        if (is_digit(*hex))    /* '0' - '9' */
          *decimal = *decimal* 16 + to_decimal(*hex);

        else                         /* 'A' - 'F' */
          *decimal = *decimal* 16 + 10 + *hex - 'A';

        hex++;                     /* get the next character */
      }
```

```
       else
            return (-1);              /* invalid character */
     }

   return (NO_ERROR);
   }
```

```
/*
 * NAME: octal_string_to_decimal (octal, decimal)
 *
 * FUNCTION: Converts a string containing an ASCII representation
 *           of an octal number to the corresponding decimal
 *           value.
 *
 * EXAMPLE: val = octal_string_to_decimal ("77", &decimal);
 *
 * VARIABLES USED: octal: pointer to the character string containing
 *                        the ASCII representation of the  octal value.
 *                 decimal: decimal equivalent.
 *
 * MACROS USED: is_octal(); returns TRUE if the letter is an
 *                        ASCII representation of an
 *                        octal number, otherwise FALSE
 *                        is returned.
 *              to_decimal(); converts an ASCII digit '0' - '9'
 *                        to its decimal value.
 *
 * PSEUDO CODE: initialize decimal value to 0
 *
 *              while (*octal is not NULL)
 *                  if (*octal is octal)
 *                      convert it to decimal
 *                      add the converted value to decimal
 *                      increment octal to point to the
 *                        next character in the string
 *
 *                  else
 *                      return (-1)  /* invalid character */
 *
 *              return (NO_ERROR)
 *
 */
octal_string_to_decimal (oct, decimal)
  char *oct;
  int *decimal;  /* decimal equivalent */
  {
   *decimal = 0;

   /* as long as the character in *octal is a valid octal
      value, convert it to decimal, otherwise return -1 */

   while (*oct)
```

```
      if (is_octal(*oct))
        *decimal = *decimal * 8 + to_decimal(*oct++);

      else
        return(-1);   /* invalid character */

    return (NO_ERROR);
  }
```

```
/*
 * NAME: binary_string_to_decimal (binary, decimal)
 *
 * FUNCTION: Converts a string containing an ASCII representation
 *           of a binary number to the corresponding decimal
 *           value.
 *
 * EXAMPLE: val = binary_string_to_decimal ("110011", &decimal);
 *
 * VARIABLES USED: binary: pointer to the character string containing
 *                         the ASCII representation of the binary
 *                         value.
 *                 decimal: decimal equivalent.
 *
 * MACROS USED: is_binary(); returns TRUE if the letter is an
 *                         ASCII representation of a
 *                         binary number, otherwise FALSE
 *                         is returned.
 *              to_decimal(); converts an ASCII digit '0' - '9'
 *                         to its decimal value.
 *
 * PSEUDO CODE: initialize decimal value to 0
 *
 *              while (*binary is not NULL)
 *                if (*binary is binary)
 *                    convert it to decimal
 *                    add the converted value to decimal
 *                    increment binary to point to the
 *                       next character in the string
 *
 *                else
 *                    return (-1)  /* invalid character */
 *
 *              return (NO_ERROR)
 *
 */
binary_string_to_decimal (binary, decimal)
  char *binary;
  int *decimal;
  {
  *decimal = 0; /* decimal representation */

  /* as long as the character in *binary is a valid binary
     value, convert it to decimal, otherwise return -1 */
```

```
  while (*binary)

    if (is_binary(*binary))
        *decimal = *decimal * 2 + to_decimal(*binary++);

    else
        return(-1);    /* invalid character */

  return (NO_ERROR);
}
```

```
/*
 * NAME: decimal_to_octal (decimal)
 *
 * FUNCTION: Converts a decimal value to its corresponding octal
 *           value.
 *
 * EXAMPLE: val = decimal_to_octal (decimal);
 *
 * VARIABLES USED: decimal: contains the decimal value to
 *                          convert to octal.
 *                 octal: octal equivalent.
 *                 count: counter.
 *
 * MACROS USED: abs_val(); returns the absolute value of a value.
 *              remainder(); returns the remainder of an integer
 *                           division between two values.
 *
 * ROUTINES CALLED: power(); returns the result of a value raised
 *                           to the power specified.
 *
 * PSEUDO CODE: convert the decimal value to octal as follows:
 *
 *              assume decimal = 125
 *
 *              125 / 8 => 15 R  5
 *
 *              15 / 8  =>  1 R  7
 *
 *               1 / 8  =>  0 R  1
 *
 *        the remainders 1 7 5 produce the octal equivalent (175)
 *
 */
decimal_to_octal (dec)
  int dec;
{
  int octal = 0; /* octal equivalent */
  int count;

  for (count = 0; (dec / 8.0) != 0; count++)
    {
      octal = abs_val(octal) + remainder(dec, 8) * power (10.0, count);
```

```
      dec = dec / 8;
   }

 return (octal);  /* octal equivalent */
 }
```

```
/*
 * NAME: dec_to_hex (decimal)
 *
 * FUNCTION: Converts a decimal value to its corresponding hexadecimal
 *           value.
 *
 * EXAMPLE: val = dec_to_hex (decimal);
 *
 * VARIABLES USED: decimal: contains the decimal value to convert
 *                          to hexadecimal.
 *                 hex: hexadecimal equivalent.
 *                 count: counter.
 *
 * MACROS USED: abs_val(); returns the absolute value of a value.
 *              remainder(); returns the remainder of an integer
 *                           division between two values.
 *
 * ROUTINES CALLED: power(); returns the result of a value raised
 *                           to the power specified.
 *
 * PSEUDO CODE: convert the decimal value in decimal to hexadecimal
 *              as follows:
 *
 *              assume decimal = 125
 *
 *              125 / 16  =>   7 R 12
 *
 *                7 / 16  =>   0 R  7
 *
 *         the remainders 7 12 are the hex equivalent (7D)
 *
 */
dec_to_hex (dec)
  unsigned int dec;
 {
  unsigned int hex = 0;  /* hexadecimal equivalent */
  int count;

  for (count = 0; (dec / 16.0) != 0; count++)
   {
     hex = hex + remainder(dec, 16) * power (10.0, count);
     dec = dec / 16;
   }

  return (hex);   /* hexadecimal equivalent */
 }
```

```
/*
 * NAME: hex_to_dec (hex)
 *
 * FUNCTION: Converts a hexadecimal value to its corresponding decimal
 *           value.
 *
 * EXAMPLE: val = hex_to_dec (hex);
 *
 * VARIABLES USED: hex: contains the hexadecimal value to convert
 *                      to decimal.
 *                 dec: decimal equivalent.
 *                 count: counter.
 *
 * MACROS USED: remainder(); returns the remainder of an integer
 *                      division.
 *
 * ROUTINES CALLED: power(); returns the result of a value raised
 *                      to the power specified.
 *
 * PSEUDO CODE: convert the hexadecimal value to decimal as follows:
 *
 *              assume hex = 123
 *
 *              3 * power (16, 0) ==>   3
 *              2 * power (16, 1) ==>  32
 *              1 * power (16, 2) ==> 256
 *                                    ---
 *                                    301
 *
 */
hex_to_decimal (hex)
 unsigned int hex;
 {
 unsigned int dec = 0;  /* decimal equivalent */
 int count;

 for (count = 0; hex / 10.0; count++)
   {
    dec = dec + remainder(hex, 10) * power (16.0, count);

    hex = hex / 10;
   }

 return (dec);  /* decimal equivalent */
}
```

```
/*
 * NAME: octal_to_dec (octal)
 *
 * FUNCTION: Converts an octal value to its corresponding decimal
 *           value.
 *
 * EXAMPLE: val = octal_to_dec (octal);
 *
```

```
 * VARIABLES USED: octal: contains the octal value to convert
 *                        to decimal.
 *                 dec: decimal equivalent.
 *                 count: counter.
 *
 * MACROS USED: remainder(); returns the remainder of an integer
 *                           division.
 *
 * ROUTINES CALLED: power(); returns the result of a value raised
 *                           to the power specified.
 *
 * PSEUDO CODE: convert the octal value to decimal as follows:
 *
 *              assume octal = 123
 *
 *              3 * power (8, 0) ==>    3
 *              2 * power (8, 1) ==>   16
 *              1 * power (8, 2) ==>   64
 *                                    ---
 *                                     83   decimal equivalent
 *
 */

int octal_to_decimal (oct)
  int oct;
 {
  int dec = 0;    /* decimal equivalent */
  int count;

  for (count = 0; oct / 10.0; count++)
   {
    dec = dec + remainder(oct, 10) * power (8.0, count);

    oct = oct / 10;
   }

  return (dec);  /* decimal equivalent */
 }
```

```
/*
 * NAME: to_hexadecimal_string (decimal, hex)
 *
 * FUNCTION: Converts an unsigned decimal value to the corresponding
 *           ASCII representation of the value in hexadecimal.
 *
 * EXAMPLE: to_hexadecimal_string (10, hex); assigns hex the letter "A".
 *
 * VARIABLES USED: decimal: contains the decimal value to convert
 *                          to the hexadecimal string.
 *                 hex: string containing the hexadecimal equivalent.
 *                 index: index into the character string.
 *
 * MACROS USED: remainder(); returns the remainder of an integer
 *                           division.
```

```
*                   to_ascii(); converts a number in the range 0 - 9 to
*                             its equivalent ASCII representation.
*
* ROUTINES CALLED: power(); returns the result of a value raised
*                           to the power specified.
*                   string_rev(); reverses the contents of a string.
*                   remainder(); returns the remainder of an integer
*                             division.
*
* PSEUDO CODE: Convert the decimal value to hexadecimal via the
*              algorithm provided in dec_to_hex()
*
*              Convert the hexadecimal value to ASCII and place it
*              into the string hex
*
*              Reverse the string so that the letters are in the proper
*              order.  if the number is 155, the conversion places
*              it into the array as 551 so the string must be reversed
*/

to_hexadecimal_string (dec, hex)
  unsigned int dec;                  /* decimal value */
  char hex[];                        /* hexadecimal string */
{
  int index = 0;
  int value;

  if (dec == 0)                      /* check for a value of zero */
   hex [index++] = to_ascii(0);

  while (dec / 16.0 != 0)
   {
    value = remainder(dec, 16);

    if (value < 10)                              /* 0 - 9 */
      hex [index++] = to_ascii(value);

    else                                         /* A - F */
      hex [index++] = value - 10 + 'A';

    dec = dec / 16;
   }

  hex[index] = NULL;

  /* reverse the string */

  string_rev (hex, 0, index);
}
```

```
/*
* NAME: to_octal_string (decimal, octal)
*
* FUNCTION: Converts an unsigned decimal value to the corresponding
*           ASCII representation of the value in octal.
*
```

```
 *  EXAMPLE: to_octal_string (10, octal); assigns octal
 *                                     the letters "12".
 *
 *  VARIABLES USED: decimal: contains the decimal value to convert
 *                           to the octal string.
 *                  octal: string containing the octal equivalent.
 *                  index: index into the character string.
 *
 *  MACROS USED: remainder(); returns the remainder of an integer
 *                            division.
 *               to_ascii(); converts a number in the range 0 - 9 to
 *                           its equivalent ASCII representation.
 *
 *  ROUTINES CALLED: power(); returns the result of a value raised
 *                           to the power specified.
 *                   string_rev(); reverses the contents of a string.
 *
 *  PSEUDO CODE: Convert the decimal value to octal via the
 *               algorithm provided in dec_to_octal()
 *
 *               Convert the octal value to ASCII and place it into
 *               the string octal
 *
 *               Reverse the string so the letters are in the proper
 *               order.  if the number is 155, the conversion places
 *               it into the array as 551 so the string must be reversed
 */
to_octal_string (dec, oct)
  unsigned int dec;              /* decimal value */
  char oct[];                    /* octal string */
  {
  int index = 0;

  if (dec == 0)                  /* check for a value of zero */
   oct [index++] = to_ascii(0);

  while (dec / 8.0 != 0)
   {
    oct[index++] = to_ascii(remainder(dec, 8));

    dec = dec / 8;
   }

  oct[index] = NULL;

  /* reverse the string */
  string_rev (oct, 0, index);
 }
```

```
/*
 *  NAME: to_binary_string (decimal, binary)
 *
 *  FUNCTION: Converts an unsigned decimal value to the corresponding
 *            ASCII representation of the value in binary.
 *
```

```
*  EXAMPLE: to_binary_string (10, binary); assigns binary
*                                    the letters "0111".
*
*  VARIABLES USED: decimal: contains the decimal value to convert
*                           to the binary string.
*                  octal: string containing the binary equivalent.
*                  index: index into the character string.
*
*  MACROS USED: remainder(); returns the remainder of an integer
*                            division.
*               to_ascii(); converts a number in the range 0 - 9 to
*                           its equivalent ASCII representation.
*
*  ROUTINES CALLED: power(); returns the result of a value raised
*                            to the power specified.
*
*  PSEUDO CODE: Convert the decimal value to binary via the
*               algorithm provided below:
*
*               decimal contains 7
*
*                   7 / 2 ==> 3 R 1
*                   3 / 2 ==> 1 R 1
*                   1 / 2 ==> 0 R 1
*
*               The remainders 1 1 1 produce the binary equivalent (111)
*
*               Convert the binary value to ASCII and place it into
*               the string binary.
*
*               Reverse the string so the letters are in the proper
*               order.  if the number is 11001, the conversion places it
*               into the array as 10011 so the string must be reversed
*/

to_binary_string (dec, binary)
  unsigned int dec;              /* decimal value */
  char binary[];                 /* binary string */
{
  int index = 0;
  int count = 0;

  while (dec / 2.0 != 0)
   {
    binary[index++] = to_ascii(remainder(dec, 2));

    dec = dec / 2;
    count++;
   }

  /* pad the string with zeros - 10001 => 0000000000010001 */

  while (count++ <= 15)
    binary [index++] = '0';

  binary[index] = NULL;

  /* reverse the contents of the string */
```

```
  string_rev (binary, 0, index);
}
```

C H A P T E R

10

File Manipulation Programs

A major factor affecting software development is the programming tools available for manipulating and extracting data from files. This chapter uses the generic tools developed in Chapters 2 through 9 to implement several file manipulation routines that are not present in most operating systems. For example, how many times have you made a minor change to a program, only to have the compiler detect a misspelled word in the file? Rather than having to reenter the editor, you can replace or delete each occurrence of the word within the file with the **replace** routine.

This chapter also includes routines that append files, view specific lines in a file, display the lines that differ between two files, extract specific lines from one file and write them to another file, and even encrypt a file for protection from other users. Since these programs use routines that you have previously developed, the programs are quite readable. It is still recommended, however, that you use debug write statements within each program to increase your understanding.

In addition to providing useful program development tools, the routines in this chapter introduce several concepts that are critical to the development of generic C utilities, namely the use of command-line arguments and qualifiers within the command line. Each program presented in this chapter is introduced in the following order:

1. Calling sequence
2. Documentation
3. C source code.

The calling sequence illustrates the actual command entered to invoke the program. Many of the programs support the use of optional output files that are represented in the calling sequence within brackets. For example:

```
tab input_file [output_file]
```

The documentation for each routine includes a description of the variables used, the macros used, the functions called, and the pseudo code. In addition, several of the programs are accompanied by examples that should help you understand the actual processing before you begin examining the C source code. Keep in mind that you can modify these routines to suit your purposes.

Command-Line Arguments

The ability to pass command-line arguments into a program is one of the most powerful capabilities provided by C. When a command line is passed to a program, two parameters are passed to **main( )**:

```
main (argc, argv)
```

These parameters are treated no differently from the parameters passed to other functions and must therefore be declared prior to the start of the routine.

```
main (argc, argv)
  int argc;          /* number of arguments */
  char *argv[];      /* actual arguments */
{

  /* remainder of the code */

}
```

The parameter **argc** contains the number of command-line arguments. The parameter **argv[ ]** is an array of pointers to character strings that contain the actual command-line arguments. Consider the following command line:

append file1 file2

argc is assigned 3 since there are three command-line arguments. The elements in **argv[ ]** point to the following character strings:

argv[0] pointer to "append"
argv[1] pointer to "file1"
argv[2] pointer to "file2"
argv[3] pointer to NULL

The following routine displays the command-line arguments passed to a program:

```
/*
 * NAME: display_command_line (argv)
 *
 * FUNCTION: Displays the command line entered.
 *
 * EXAMPLE: display_command_line (argv);
 *
 * VARIABLES USED: argv: array of character strings to the command
 *                       line arguments.
 *
 * PSEUDO CODE: while (the value in argv is not NULL)
 *                  print the value
 *                  increment argv to point to the next
 *                  command line argument
 *
 *              return
 *
 */
```

```
display_command_line (argv)
  char *argv[];
{
  while (*argv)
    printf ("%s ", *argv++);

  putchar(NEWLINE);
}
```

The UNIX operating system provides a program similar to this routine, called **echo**, which displays the command-line arguments passed to the program. The reason for implementing the routine as a function is to use it as a debugging tool in other routines. The following program uses **display—command—line ( )** to print the command line.

```
main (argc, argv)
   int argc;        /* count of the command line arguments */
   char *argv[];    /* actual command line arguments */
{

   display_command_line (argv);

}
```

Pointers and command-line arguments are two of the most powerful tools you can use in your routines. The programs in the remainder of this chapter make extensive use of them.

Output files are optional with most commands so you can first view how the command line entered will affect the input file before you write it to the output file. Once you are satisfied with the results, you can specify the output file.

The Append program appends one file to another. For example, if **file1** contains

this is line 1
this is it
line 3 of the file
this line is very long
line 5 of the file

six six six six
this is line 7
line 8
last line

and **file2** contains

new1
new2
new3

the command

```
append file2 file1
```

will modify file 1 as follows:

this is line 1
this is it
line 3 of the file
this line is very long
line 5 of the file
six six six six
this is line 7
line 8
last line
new1
new2
new3

```
/*
 * NAME: append.c
 *
 * FUNCTION: Appends the first file in the command line
 *           to the second file specified.
 *
```

```
*  ROUTINES CALLED: strings_are_equal(); returns TRUE if two strings
*                                        are equal, otherwise FALSE
*                                        is returned.
*                   fwriteln(); writes a line to a file insuring that
*                               only one newline character is written.
*
*  VARIABLES USED: input_file: pointer to the input file.
*                  output_file: pointer to the output file.
*                  argv: array of pointers to the command line.
*                  argc: number of command line arguments.
*
*  PSEUDO CODE: if (enough command line arguments aren't present)
*                  print an error message
*                  exit to the operating system
*
*               if (the input and output file names are the same)
*                  print an error message
*                  exit to the operating system -- most micro computer
*                     operating systems will not allow us to open the
*                     same file twice
*
*               if (either file cannot be opened)
*                  print an error message
*                  exit to the operating system
*
*               while (the file to append contains lines)
*                  get a line from the file
*                  append it to the second file
*
*               close the files
*
*/

#include <stdio.h>        /* contains definitions for file I/O */
#include "defn.h"
#include "strings.h"
#include "fwriteln.c"      /* contains the routine fwriteln() */
#include "strequal.c"      /* contains the routine strings_are_equal() */

main (argc, argv)
  int argc;                /* number of command line arguments */
  char *argv[];            /* array of pointers to the command line */
  {
  FILE *input_file;        /* file appended onto the output_file */
  FILE *output_file;
  FILE *fopen ();

  char string[MAX_STRING];    /* string read from the file */

  if (argc < 3)          /* see if the file names are present */
    {
    printf ("append: invalid useage: append file1 file2\n");
    printf ("append: will append file1 to file2\n");
```

```
    exit (1);
  }

/* see if the file was successfully opened and, if so, append
 * the lines it contains to the output file, otherwise print
 * an error message.
 */

else if ((input_file = fopen (argv[1], "r")) == NULL)
  {
   printf ("append: error opening file %s\n", argv[1]);
   exit (1);
  }

/* insure that the output file is different from the input file */

if (strings_are_equal (argv[1], argv[2]))
   {
    printf ("append: input and output file must differ\n");
    exit (1);
   }

else if ((output_file = fopen (argv[2], "a")) == NULL)
   {
    printf ("append: error opening file %s\n", argv[2]);
    exit (1);
   }

/* append the lines of the input file to the output file */

while (fgets (string, MAX_STRING, input_file))
    fwriteln (output_file, string);

/* close the files */

fclose (input_file);
fclose (output_file);
}
```

The Filecase program changes the letters contained within a file to either uppercase or lowercase as specified in the command line. The true function of Filecase is to introduce the concept of command-line qualifiers. The calling sequence for Filecase is

```
filecase -qualifier filename [output_file]
```

The two qualifiers supported by Filecase are:

   -1   directs the program to convert letters to lowercase
   -u   directs the program to convert letters to uppercase.

If **file1** contains

> this is line 1
> this is it
> line 3 of the file
> this line is very long
> line 5 of the file
> six six six six
> this is line 7
> line 8
> last line

and Filecase is invoked with

```
filecase -u file1
```

the screen will display the following:

> THIS IS LINE 1
> THIS IS IT
> LINE 3 OF THE FILE
> THIS LINE IS VERY LONG
> LINE 5 OF THE FILE
> SIX SIX SIX SIX
> THIS IS LINE 7
> LINE 8
> LAST LINE

To convert the letters contained in **file1** to lowercase and write the output to the file **case.dat**, the calling sequence would be

```
filecase -l file1 case.dat
```

```
/*
 * NAME: filecase.c
 *
 * FUNCTION: Converts the contents of a file to either UPPER or
 *           lowercase based upon the qualifier -u or -l in the
 *           command line.
 *
```

```
 *  ROUTINES CALLED: fwriteln(); writes a line to a file and insures
 *                              that only one newline character is
 *                              written.
 *                   strings_are_equal(); returns TRUE if two strings
 *                              are equal, otherwise FALSE
 *                              is returned.
 *                   str_index(); returns the starting location of a
 *                              substring within a string, or -1 if
 *                              the substring was not present.
 *                   change_file_case(): converts the file to the case
 *                              specified, and writes it to
 *                              the output destination (file
 *                              or stdout).
 *
 *  VARIABLES USED: lowercase: TRUE if we are converting letters
 *                            to lowercase.
 *                  input_file: pointer to the input file.
 *                  output_file: pointer to the output file.
 *                  argv: array of pointers to the command line.
 *                  argc: number of command line arguments.
 *
 *  PSEUDO CODE: if (enough command line arguments are not present)
 *                  print an error message
 *                  exit to the operating system
 *
 *               if (the qualifier entered is not valid) (-u or -l)
 *                  print an error message
 *                  exit to the operating system
 *
 *               if (the input and output files are the same)
 *                  print an error message
 *                  exit to the operating system -- most micro
 *                    computer operating system will not allow
 *                    us to open the same file twice
 *
 *               if (argc < 4)           -- no output was file specified
 *                  output_file = stdout
 *
 *               if (either of the files cannot be opened)
 *                  print an error message
 *                  exit to the operating system
 *
 *               invoke change_file_case() to change the case of the
 *                  contents of the file
 *
 *               close the file(s)
 *
 */

#include <stdio.h>      /* contains definitions for file I/O */
#include "defn.h"
#include "strings.h"

#include "fwriteln.c" /* contains the routine fwriteln() */
#include "strindex.c" /* contains the routine str_index() */
#include "strequal.c" /* contains the routine strings_are_equal() */
#include "case.c"      /* contains the routines string_to_uppercase() */
                       /* and string_to_lowercase() */
```

```
main (argc, argv)
  int argc;              /* number of command line arguments */
  char *argv[];          /* array of pointers to the command line */
{
  FILE *input_file;      /* file to change the case of */
  FILE *output_file;     /* file to write the changes to or stdout */
  FILE *fopen ();

  int lowercase;              /* TRUE if user wants lowercase letters */

  if (argc < 3)              /* see if the input file name is present */
   {
    printf ("filecase: invalid useage: filecase -u or -l file [file]\n");
    exit (1);
   }

  /* find out if user wants UPPER or lowercase for file */

  if (str_index ("-l-L", argv[1]) != -1)
    lowercase = TRUE;

  else if (str_index ("-u-U", argv[1]) != -1)
    lowercase = FALSE;

  else
   {
    printf ("filecase: invalid qualifier %s\n", argv[1]);
    printf ("filecase: use -l or -u\n");
    exit (1);
   }

  /* make sure that the input and output files are different */

  if (strings_are_equal (argv[2], argv[3]))
   {
    printf ("filecase: input and output files must differ\n");
    exit (1);
   }

  /* see if the file was successfully opened and, if so, convert
   * the lines it contains to the proper case and print them,
   * otherwise print an error message.
   */

  if ((input_file = fopen (argv[2], "r")) == NULL)
   {
    printf ("filecase: error opening file %s\n", argv[2]);
    exit (1);
   }

  if (argc < 4)
    output_file = stdout; /* no output file was specified */

  /* insure that the output file is different from the input file */

  else if (strings_are_equal (argv[3], argv[2]))
   {
    printf ("filecase: input file and output must differ\n");
```

```
     exit (1);
   }

  else if ((output_file = fopen (argv[3], "w")) == NULL)
   {
    printf ("filecase: error opening file %s\n", argv[3]);
    exit (1);
   }

  /* change the case of the letters in the file */

  change_file_case (input_file, output_file, lowercase);

  fclose (input_file);

  if (argc == 4)            /* if the output is to stdout */
    fclose (output_file);   /* don't close a file */
}




/*
 * NAME: change_file_case (input_file, output_file, lowercase)
 *
 * FUNCTION: Converts the characters in a file to either UPPER
 *           or lowercase.
 *
 * EXAMPLE: change_file_case (argv[1], argv[2], lowercase);
 *
 * VARIABLES USED: input_file: pointer to the input file.
 *                 output_file: pointer to the output file.
 *                 lowercase: TRUE if the file is to be converted
 *                            to lowercase, otherwise the characters
 *                            are converted to UPPERCASE.
 *
 * ROUTINES CALLED: fwriteln(); writes a line to file insuring
 *                             that only one newline character
 *                             is written.
 *                  str_to_lowercase(); converts the contents of a
 *                                      string to lowercase.
 *                  str_to_uppercase(); converts the contents of a
 *                                      string to UPPERCASE.
 *
 * PSEUDO CODE: while (there are lines in the input file)
 *                  get a line a from the file
 *                  if (convert to lowercase is TRUE)
 *                      convert the string to lowercase
 *                  else
 *                      convert the string to UPPERCASE
 *
 *                  write the converted string to the output file
 *
 *              return -- the file case is changed
 *
 */

change_file_case (input_file, output_file, lowercase)
  FILE *input_file;
```

```
FILE *output_file;
int lowercase;        /* if TRUE convert the letters to lowercase
                         otherwise convert them to UPPERCASE */
{
 char string [MAX_STRING];  /* buffer for lines read from the file */

 while (fgets (string, MAX_STRING, input_file))
    {
     if (lowercase)
       str_to_lowercase (string);

     else
       str_to_uppercase (string);

     fwriteln (output_file, string);
    }
}
```

The program First displays the lines starting at the beginning of a file. This program is similar to the UNIX utility **head**. For example, if **file1** contains

this is line 1
this is it
line 3 of the file
this line is very long
line 5 of the file
six six six six
this is line 7
line 8
last line

the command line

```
first 3 file1
```

will display the first three lines of **file1** on the screen.

this is line 1
this is it
line 3 of the file

To write the first five lines contained in **file1** to the file **first.dat**, enter the command line

```
first 5 file1 first.dat
```

If the number of lines is not specified, the default value is 10. For
example, the command

```
first file1
```

displays the first ten lines in **file1**. Since **file1** contains only eight
lines, First will stop displaying lines when the end-of-file is found.
The calling sequence for First is

```
first [# of lines] file [output_file]
```

```
/*
 * NAME: first.c
 *
 * FUNCTION: Displays the number of lines specified in the command line
 *           starting with the first line in the file.  If no lines are
 *           specified, first will display 10 lines by default.
 *
 * ROUTINES CALLED: strings_are_equal(); returns TRUE if the two strings
 *                                       are equal, otherwise FALSE is
 *                                       returned.
 *                  int_convert(); converts a string to the corresponding
 *                                 integer value.
 *                  file_line_count(); returns the number of lines in a
 *                                     file.
 *                  display_command_line(); displays the command line
 *                                          entered to invoke the program.
 *
 * VARIABLES USED: input_file: pointer to the input file.
 *                 output_file: pointer to the output destination (file
 *                              or stdout).
 *                 file_length: number of lines in the file to display.
 *                 lines_present: TRUE if the number of lines to
 *                                display is specified.
 *                 input_index: index into argv[] of the name of the
 *                              input file.
 *                 output_index: index into argv[] of the name of the
 *                               output file.
 *                 string: line read from the file.
 *                 count: counter.
 *                 number_of_lines: number of lines to display.
 *
 * PSEUDO CODE: if (enough command line arguments are not present)
 *                 print an error message (should be: first file)
 *                 exit to the operating system
 *
 *              if (argv[1] can be converted to an integer)
 *                 number of lines to print = int_convert(argv[1])
 *                 input_index = 2 -- location in argv[] of the
 *                                    name of the input file
```

```
*             else
*                 number of lines to print = 10 by default
*
*             if (argc > 3) -- the number of lines to display
*                     is present
*                 increment output_index to point to the name of
*                     the output file in argv[]
*
*             (since the number  of lines to display is in argv[]
*             we must offset the location in argv[] of the input
*             and output files by one)
*
*             get the length of the file to display
*
*             if (the input file and output file are the same)
*               print an error message
*               exit to the operating system -- most micro computer
*                   operating systems will not allow us to open the
*                   same file twice
*
*             if (argc < 3 or argc == 3 and the number of lines
*                 to display is present)
*               output_file = stdout  (no output file specified)
*
*             if (either of the files cannot be opened)
*               print an error message
*               exit to the operating system
*
*             if (the number of lines to display is > the
*                 number of lines in the file)
*               assign the number of lines to display the length
*                   of the file so we don't try to read past the
*                   End Of File (EOF)
*
*             initialize count = 0
*             while (count < the number of lines to display)
*               get a line from the file
*               write it to the output destination
*               increment count
*
*             close the file(s)
*
*/

#include <stdio.h>      /* contains definitions for file I/O */
#include "defn.h"
#include "strings.h"
#include "fwriteln.c" /* contains the routine fwriteln() */
#include "filelen.c"  /* contains the routine file_line_count() */
#include "intcvrt.c"  /* contains the routine int_convert() */
#include "strequal.c" /* contains the routine strings_are_equal() */
#include "echo.c"     /* contains the routine display_command_line() */

main (argc, argv)
  int argc;             /* number of command line arguments */
  char *argv[];         /* array of pointers to the command line */
  {
```

```
FILE *input_file;     /* input file to display */
FILE *output_file;    /* file written to, or stdout */
FILE *fopen ();

int file_length;           /* number of lines in the input file */
int count;                 /* counter */
int number_of_lines = 10;  /* default value */

int input_index = 1;       /* location of the name of the input
                              file in argv[] */
int output_index = 2;      /* location of the name of the output
                              file in argv[] */

int lines_present = FALSE;  /* TRUE if the user specified the
                               number of lines to display */

int opened_output_file = FALSE; /* was output to a file or stdout */

char string[MAX_STRING];        /* string read from the file */

if (argc < 2)                   /* see if a file name is present */
 {
  printf ("first: no file specified\n");
  exit (1);
 }

if (argc >= 3)          /* see if the number of lines is present */

   if (int_convert (argv[1], &number_of_lines) == IO_ERROR)
       number_of_lines = 10;            /* by default */

   else if (argc > 3)   /* first # file file */
       {
         lines_present = TRUE;

   /* since the number of lines is present, the location of the
      names of the input and output files is offset one location
      in the array argv[] */

         input_index = 2;   /* location of the file names in argv[] */
         output_index = 3;
       }

   else   /* first # file */
       {
         lines_present = TRUE;        /* number of lines specified by
                                         the user was valid */

         input_index = 2;            /* location of the name of input
                                        file in the argv[] */
       }

/* see if the file was successfully opened and, if so, count
 * the lines it contains and print the desired lines, otherwise
 * print an error message.
 */
```

```
if ((file_length = file_line_count (argv[input_index])) == ERROR)
 {
  printf ("first: error opening file %s\n", argv[input_index]);
  display_command_line (argv);
  exit (1);
 }

/* open the file for reading */

if ((input_file = fopen (argv[input_index], "r")) == NULL)
 {
  printf ("first: error opening file %s\n", argv[input_index]);
  display_command_line (argv);
  exit (1);
 }

/* if no output file is specified, print to stdout */

if (argc < 3)
  output_file = stdout;

else if (argc == 3 && lines_present)
  output_file = stdout;

/* insure the input file is different from the output file */

else if (strings_are_equal (argv[input_index], argv[output_index]))
  {
   printf ("first: input file and output file must differ\n");
   display_command_line (argv);
   exit (1);
  }

else
  {
   if ((output_file = fopen (argv[output_index], "w")) == NULL)
    {
     printf ("first: error opening file %s\n", argv[output_index]);
     display_command_line (argv);
     exit (1);
    }
   opened_output_file = TRUE;
  }

/* make sure that the number of lines to display is <= the
   number of lines in the file */

if (number_of_lines > file_length)
   number_of_lines = file_length;  /* only display to EOF */

for (count = 0; count < number_of_lines; count++)
   {
    fgets (string, MAX_STRING, input_file);
    fwriteln (output_file, string);
   }

fclose (input_file);

if (opened_output_file) /* if the output is to stdout */
   fclose (output_file); /* don't close a file */
}
```

The Last program is similar to First in that it returns specific lines from a file. However, Last will display the lines at the end of the file instead of the start. This routine is similar to the UNIX utility **tail**. For example, if **file1** contains

this is line 1
this is it
line 3 of the file
this line is very long
line 5 of the file
six six six six
this is line 7
line 8
last line

the command line

```
last  3  file1
```

will display the last three lines in **file1** on the screen:

this is line 7
line 8
last line

The calling sequence for Last is

```
last [# of lines] file [output file]
```

If you do not specify the number of lines to be displayed, Last will display ten lines by default. For the UNIX or MS-DOS operating systems this sequence would be

```
last [# of lines] file > output
```

```
/*
 * NAME: last.c
 *
 * FUNCTION: Displays the number of lines specified in the command
 *           line starting at the last line in the file minus the
 *           number of lines to display.
 *
 *   For example, if the file contains 27 lines and the last 10 lines
 *   are desired, the first line displayed will be line 17.
```

```
*                        (27 - 10 => 17).
*
*    If no lines are specified, last will display the last 10 lines
*    in the file by default.
*
* ROUTINES CALLED: strings_are_equal(); returns TRUE if the two strings
*                                       are equal, otherwise FALSE is
*                                       returned.
*                  int_convert(); converts a string to the corresponding
*                                 integer value.
*                  file_line_count(); returns the number of lines in a
*                                     file.
*                  display_command_line(); displays the command line
*                                          entered to invoke the program.
*
* VARIABLES USED: input_file: pointer to the input file.
*                 output_file: pointer to the output destination (file
*                              or stdout).
*                 file_length: number of lines in the file to display.
*                 lines_present: TRUE if number of lines to display
*                                is specified.
*                 input_index: index into argv[] of the name of the
*                              input file.
*                 output_index: index into argv[] of the name of the
*                               output file.
*                 string: line read from the file.
*                 count: counter.
*                 number_of_lines: number of lines to display.
*
* PSEUDO CODE: if (enough command line arguments are not present)
*                  print an error message (should be: last file)
*                  exit to the operating system
*
*              if (argv[1] can be converted to an integer)
*                  number of lines to print = int_convert(argv[1])
*                  input_index = 2 -- location in argv[] of the
*                                     name of the input file
*              else
*                  number of lines to print = 10 by default
*
*              if (argc > 3) -- number of lines to display is present
*                  increment output_index to point to the name of the
*                      output file in argv[]
*
*               (since the number of lines to display is in argv[] we
*               must offset the location in argv[] of the names of the
*               input and output files by one)
*
*              get the length of the file to display
*
*              if (the input and output file are the same)
*                 print an error message
*                 exit to the operating system -- most micro computer
*                   operating systems will not allow us to open the
*                   same file twice
*
*              if (argc < 3 or (argc == 3 and the number of lines to
*                  display is present))
*                     output_file = stdout  (no output file specified)
*
```

```
*                      if (the file(s) cannot be opened)
*                         print an error message
*                         exit to the operating system
*
*                      if (the number of lines to display is > the
*                          number of lines in the file)
*                            assign number of lines to display to the length
*                            of the file to insure that we don't try to read
*                            past the End Of the File (EOF)
*
*                      -- read the lines in the file which preceed the first
*                         line to be displayed
*
*                      initialize count = 0
*                      while (count < the file length minus the number
*                             of lines to display)
*                         get a line from the file
*                         increment count
*
*                      -- read and display the desired lines --
*
*                      set count = 0
*                      while (count < number_of_lines to display)
*                         get a line from the file
*                         write it to the output destination
*                         increment count
*
*                      close the file(s)
*
*/

#include <stdio.h>       /* contains definitions for file I/O */
#include "defn.h"
#include "strings.h"
#include "fwriteln.c"     /* contains the routine fwriteln() */
#include "filelen.c"      /* contains the routine file_line_count() */
#include "intcvrt.c"      /* contains the routine int_convert() */
#include "strequal.c"     /* contains the routine strings_are_equal() */
#include "echo.c"         /* contains the routine display_command_line() */

main (argc, argv)
  int argc;               /* number of command line arguments */
  char *argv[];           /* array of pointers to the command line */
{
  FILE *input_file;       /* input file to display */
  FILE *output_file;      /* file to be written to or stdout */
  FILE *fopen ();

  int file_length;            /* number of lines in the input file */
  int count;                  /* counter */
  int number_of_lines = 10;   /* default value */

  int input_index = 1;        /* location of the name of the input file
                                 in the array argv[] */
  int output_index = 2;       /* location of the name of the output file
                                 in the array argv[] */

  int lines_present = FALSE;   /* TRUE if the user specified the number
                                  of lines to display */
```

```
int opened_output_file = FALSE; /* TRUE if the output is to a file */

char string[MAX_STRING];         /* string read from the file */

if (argc < 2)        /* see if the input file name is present */
 {
  printf ("last: no file specified\n");
  exit (1);
 }

if (argc >= 3)        /* check if the user specified the number of
                         lines to display */

   if (int_convert (argv[1], &number_of_lines) == IO_ERROR)
      number_of_lines = 10;            /* by default */

   else if (argc > 3)  /* last # file file */
      {
       lines_present = TRUE;

 /* since the number of lines to display is present, the
    location of the names of the input and output files is
    offset one location in the array argv[] */

       input_index = 2;   /* location in argv[] of the file names */
       output_index = 3;
      }

   else  /* last # file */
      {
       lines_present = TRUE;  /* the number of lines specified by
                                 the user was valid */
       input_index = 2;       /* location of the input file
                                 name in argv[] */

      }

 /* see if the file was successfully opened and, if so, count
  * the lines it contains and print the desired lines, otherwise
  * print an error message.
  */

if ((file_length = file_line_count (argv[input_index])) == ERROR)
 {
  printf ("last: error opening file %s\n", argv[input_index]);
  display_command_line (argv);
  exit (1);
 }

 /* open the file for reading */

if ((input_file = fopen (argv[input_index], "r")) == NULL)
 {
  printf ("last: error opening file %s\n", argv[input_index]);
  display_command_line (argv);
  exit (1);
 }
```

```
/* if no output file is specified, print to stdout */

if (argc < 3)
  output_file = stdout;

else if (argc == 3 && lines_present) /* last # file */
  output_file = stdout;

/* insure that the output file differs from input file */

else if (strings_are_equal (argv[input_index], argv[output_index]))
  {
    printf ("last: input and output file must differ\n");
    display_command_line (argv);
    exit (1);
  }

else
  {
  if ((output_file = fopen (argv[output_index], "w")) == NULL)
    {
      printf ("last: error opening file %s\n", argv[output_index]);
      display_command_line (argv);
      exit (1);
    }
  opened_output_file = TRUE;
  }

/* make sure that the number of lines to display is <= the
   number of lines in the file */

  if (number_of_lines > file_length)
    number_of_lines = file_length;

  /* read the lines in the file which precede the first line desired
     by the user, but do not display them */

  for (count = 0; count < file_length - number_of_lines; count++)
    fgets (string, MAX_STRING, input_file);

  /* display the lines desired */

  for (count = 0; count < number_of_lines; count++)
    {
      fgets (string, MAX_STRING, input_file);
      fwriteln (output_file, string);
    }

  fclose (input_file);

  if (opened_output_file)   /* if the output is to stdout */
    fclose (output_file);   /* don't close a file */
  }
```

The Extract program combines the First and Last programs to allow lines to be extracted from any location in a file. The calling sequence for Extract is

```
extract line# line# file [output file]
```

If **file1** contains the following

    this is line 1
    this is it
    line 3 of the file
    this line is very long
    line 5 of the file
    six six six six
    this is line 7
    line 8
    last line

the command line

```
extract 1 4 file1
```

will display the contents of lines 1 through 4 of **file1** on the screen as follows:

    this is line 1
    this is it
    line 3 of the file
    this line is very long

To write the lines to **file.dat**, the command line would be

```
extract 1 4 file1 file.dat
```

```
/*
 * NAME: extract.c
 *
 * FUNCTION: Extracts a specific portion of a file and writes it to
 *           the desired output location (file or stdout).
 *
 * ROUTINES CALLED: strings_are_equal(); returns TRUE if two strings
 *                                       are equal, otherwise FALSE
 *                                       is returned.
 *
 *                  display_command_line(); displays the command line
 *                                          entered to invoke the
 *                                          program.
```

```
*                     file_line_count(); returns the number of lines
*                                   in a file.
*                     int_convert(); converts a string into an
*                                   integer value.
*
* VARIABLES USED: string: line read from the file.
*                 start_line: line number to begin extracting lines
*                             from the file at.
*                 stop_line: last line number extracted.
*                 line: current line number.
*                 input_file: pointer to the input file.
*                 output_file: pointer to the output file.
*                 length_of_file: number of lines in the file.
*                 argc: number of command line aguments.
*                 argv: array of pointers to the command line.
*
* PSEUDO CODE: if (enough command line arguments are not present)
*                    print an error message (should be: extract # # file)
*                    exit to the operating system
*
*              get the length of the file
*              if (the length of file is -1)
*                print an error message
*                exit to the operating system
*
*              if (argv[1] can be converted to an integer)
*                assign start_line = int_convert(argv[1])
*              else
*                print an error message
*                display the command line
*                exit to the operating system
*
*              if (start_line < 1)
*                print an error message
*                display the command line
*                exit to the operating system
*
*              if (argv[2] can be converted to an integer)
*                assign start_line = int_convert(argv[2])
*              else
*                print an error message
*                display the command line
*                exit to the operating system
*
*              if (stop_line < start_line)
*                print an error message
*                display the command line
*                exit to the operating system
*
*              if (the stop_line is > the number of lines
*                  in the file)
*                assign stop_line the length of the file to
*                insure that we don't try to read past the
*                end of the file (EOF)
*
*              if (argc == 4)            -- no output file specified
*                output_file = stdout
*
```

```
*               if (the input and output file are the same)
*                   print an error message
*                   display the command line
*                   exit to the operating system -- most micro
*                     computer operating systems will not allow
*                     us to open the same file twice
*
*               if (either of the files cannot be opened)
*                   print an error message
*                   display the command line
*                   exit to the operating system
*
*               initialize line = 0
*               while (line <= start_line)
*                   get a line from the file
*                   increment line
*
*               while (line <= stop_line)
*                   get a line from the file
*                   write the line to output destination
*                   increment line
*
*               close the files
*
*/

#include <stdio.h>      /* contains definitions for file I/O */
#include "defn.h"
#include "strings.h"
#include "intcvrt.c"   /* contains the routine int_convert() */
#include "filelen.c"   /* contains the routine file_line_count() */
#include "echo.c"       /* contains the routine display_command_line() */
#include "strequal.c" /* contains the routine strings_are_equal() */

main (argc, argv)
   int argc;            /* number of command line arguments */
   char *argv[];        /* array of pointers to the command line */
{
 char string[MAX_STRING];  /* line read from the file */

 int start_line;          /* first line to extract */
 int stop_line;           /* last line to extract */
 int line;                /* current line */

 int length_of_file;      /* number of lines in the file */

 FILE *fopen(), *input_file, *output_file;

 /* see if enough command line arguments are present */

 if (argc < 4)
   {
   printf ("extract: error: extract line# line# file [file]\n");
   display_command_line (argv);
   exit(1);
   }
```

```c
/* find out how many lines are in the file. if the file does
   not exist, then display an error message and exit to the
   operating system */

if ((length_of_file = file_line_count (argv[3])) == ERROR)
 {
  printf ("extract: cannot open file %s\n", argv[3]);
  exit(1);
 }

/* see if the starting location is valid (i.e. an integer value) */

if (int_convert (argv[1], &start_line) == IO_ERROR)
 {
  printf ("extract: invalid starting location specified\n");
  display_command_line (argv);
  exit(1);
 }

if (start_line < 1)
 {
  printf ("extract: invalid starting location must be >= 1\n");
  display_command_line (argv);
  exit(1);
 }

/* see if the stopping location is valid */

if (int_convert (argv[2], &stop_line) == IO_ERROR)
 {
  printf ("extract: invalid ending location specified\n");
  display_command_line (argv);
  exit (1);
 }

if (stop_line < start_line)
 {
  printf ("extract: ending line must be >=  starting line\n");
  display_command_line (argv);
  exit(1);
 }

/* make sure that the stopping line is <= length of file */

if (stop_line > length_of_file)
  stop_line = length_of_file;   /* don't read past EOF */

/* open the input file */

if ((input_file = fopen (argv[3], "r")) == NULL)
 {
  printf ("extract: error opening file %s\n", argv[3]);
  exit (1);
 }

/* find out if an output file is specified */
```

```
if (argc == 4)              /* extract # # file */
  output_file = stdout;   /* display the file to standard output */

/* insure that the input file is different from the output file */

else if (strings_are_equal (argv[4], argv[3]))
 {
  printf ("extract: input and output files must differ\n");
  exit (1);
 }

else if ((output_file = fopen (argv[4], "w")) == NULL)
 {
  printf ("extract: cannot open file %s\n", argv[4]);
  exit(1);
 }

/* read the lines prior to the starting location */

for (line = 1; line < start_line; line++)
 fgets (string, MAX_STRING, input_file);

/* write the lines desired */

for (line = start_line; line <= stop_line; line++)
 {
  fgets (string, MAX_STRING, input_file);
  fputs (string, output_file);
 }


fclose (input_file);   /* close the input file.
                          if the output is to a file and
                          not stdout close it also */
 if (argc > 4)
  fclose (output_file);
}
```

The Remove program removes from the file the specified lines provided in the command line. The calling sequence for Remove is

```
remove starting_line# ending_line# file [output file]
```

If **file1** contains

> this is line 1
> this is it
> line 3 of the file
> this line is very long
> line 5 of the file
> six six six six

this is line 7

line 8

last line

the command line

```
remove 1 4 file1
```

will display the following on the screen:

line 5 of the file

six six six six

this is line 7

line 8

last line

To save the contents of **file1** after the lines have been removed, an output file must be declared.

```
remove 3 5 file1 remove.dat
```

```
/*
 * NAME: remove.c
 *
 * FUNCTION: Removes a specific portion of a file.
 *
 * ROUTINES CALLED: strings_are_equal(); returns TRUE if two strings
 *                                       are equal, otherwise FALSE
 *                                       is returned.
 *                  display_command_line(); displays the command line
 *                                       entered to invoke the
 *                                       program.
 *                  file_line_count(); returns the number of lines in a
 *                                       in a file.
 *                  int_convert(); converts a string to an
 *                                       integer value.
 *
 * VARIABLES USED: string: line read from the file.
 *                 start_line: line number to begin removing
 *                             lines from the file at.
 *                 stop_line: line number of the last line to be
 *                             removed.
 *                 line: current line number.
 *                 input_file: pointer to the input file.
 *                 output_file: pointer to the output file.
 *                 length_of_file: number of lines in the file.
 *                 argc: number of command line aguments.
 *                 argv: array of pointers to the command line.
 *
```

```
* PSEUDO CODE: if (enough command line arguments are not present)
*                print an error message (should be: remove # # file)
*                exit to the operating system
*
*              get the length of the file
*              if (the length of file = -1)
*                print an error message
*                exit to the operating system
*
*              if (argv[1] can be converted to an integer)
*                assign start_line = int_convert(argv[1])
*              else
*                print an error message
*                display the command line
*                exit to the operating system
*
*              if (start_line < 1)
*                print an error message
*                display the command line
*                exit to the operating system
*
*              if (argv[2] can be converted to an integer)
*                assign stop_line = int_convert(argv[2])
*              else
*                print an error message
*                display the command line
*                exit to the operating system
*
*              if (stop_line < start_line)
*                print an error message
*                display the command line
*                exit to the operating system
*
*              if (the stop_line is > to the number of lines
*                  in the file)
*                assign stop_line to the number of lines in the
*                  file to insure that we don't try to read past
*                  the end of file (EOF)
*
*              if (argc == 4)           -- no output file was specified
*                output_file = stdout
*
*              if (the input file and output file are the same)
*                print an error message
*                display the command line
*                exit to the operating system
*
*              if (either of the files cannot be opened)
*                print an error message
*                display the command line
*                exit to the operating system
*
*              -- write the lines prior to the starting location
*
*              initialize the line count to 1
*              while (the line count <= start_line)
*                get a line a line from the file
```

```
*                   write the line to output destination
*                   increment the line count
*
*           -- read the lines to remove but don't write them
*
*           while (the line count <= stop_line)
*               get a line from the file
*               increment the line count
*
*           -- write the lines remaining in the file
*
*           while (the line count <= length_of_file)
*               get a line from the file
*               write the line to the output destination
*               increment the line count
*
*           close the file(s)
*
*/

#include <stdio.h>      /* contains definitions for file I/O */
#include "defn.h"
#include "strings.h"
#include "intcvrt.c"   /* contains the routine int_convert() */
#include "filelen.c"   /* contains the routine file_line_count() */
#include "echo.c"      /* contains the routine display_command_line() */
#include "strequal.c"  /* contains the routine strngs_are_equal() */

main (argc, argv)
  int argc;              /* number of command line arguments */
  char *argv[];          /* array of pointers to the command line */
{
  char string[MAX_STRING];  /* line read from the file */

  int start_line;           /* first line to remove */
  int stop_line;            /* last line to remove */
  int line;                 /* current line displayed */

  int length_of_file;       /* number of lines in the file */

  FILE *fopen(), *input_file, *output_file;

  /* see if enough command line arguments are present */

  if (argc < 4)
   {
    printf ("remove: invalid useage: remove line# line# file [file]\n");
    display_command_line (argv);
    exit(1);
   }

  /* find out how many lines are in the file. if the file does
     not exist, then display an error message and exit to the
     operating system */

  if ((length_of_file = file_line_count (argv[3])) == ERROR)
   {
    printf ("remove: cannot open file %s\n", argv[3]);
```

```
  exit(1);
 }

/* see if the starting location is valid (i.e. an integer value) */

if (int_convert (argv[1], &start_line) == IO_ERROR)
 {
  printf ("remove: invalid starting location specified\n");
  display_command_line (argv);
  exit(1);
 }

if (start_line < 1)
 {
  printf ("remove: invalid starting location must be >= 1\n");
  display_command_line (argv);
  exit(1);
 }

/* see if the stopping location is valid */

if (int_convert (argv[2], &stop_line) == IO_ERROR)
 {
  printf ("remove: invalid ending location specified\n");
  display_command_line (argv);
  exit (1);
 }

if (stop_line < start_line)
 {
  printf ("remove: ending line must be >=  starting line\n");
  display_command_line (argv);
  exit(1);
 }

/* make sure that the stopping line is <= the length of file */

if (stop_line > length_of_file)
  stop_line = length_of_file;    /* don't read past End Of File */

if ((input_file = fopen (argv[3], "r")) == NULL)
 {
  printf ("remove: error opening file %s\n", argv[3]);
  exit (1);
 }

/* find out if an output file is specified */

if (argc == 4)              /* remove line# line# file */
  output_file = stdout;  /* display file to standard out */

/* make sure that the input and output files are not the same */

else if (strings_are_equal (argv[4], argv[3]))
 {
  printf ("remove: input and output file must differ\n");
  exit (1);
 }
```

```
else
  if ((output_file = fopen (argv[4], "w")) == NULL)
    {
     printf ("remove: cannot open file %s\n", argv[4]);
     exit(1);
    }

/* write the lines prior to the starting location */

for (line = 1; line < start_line; line++)
  {
   fgets (string, MAX_STRING, input_file);
   fputs (string, output_file);
  }


/* read the lines to be removed, but do not write them */

while (line <= stop_line)
  {
   fgets (string, MAX_STRING, input_file);
   line++;
  }

/* write the remainder of the file */

while (line++ <= length_of_file)
  {
   fgets (string, MAX_STRING, input_file);
   fputs (string, output_file);
  }

fclose (input_file);

if (argc > 4)      /* if output_file = stdout no need to close */
  fclose (output_file);
}
```

The Diff program reads and compares the contents of two files and displays the number and contents of each line that differs between the files. This program is similar to the UNIX utility **diff**. The command line for Diff is

```
diff [-stop scrolling] file1 file2
```

The optional qualifier -s directs the program to suppress scrolling of the differences. Once a screenful of information is written, the routine will stop and prompt

```
HIT <RETURN> TO CONTINUE
```

If the -s qualifier is not specified, the differences will continue to scroll past on the screen. If **file1** contains

    this is line 1
    this is it
    line 3 of the file
    this line is very long
    line 5 of the file
    six six six six
    this is line 7
    line 8
    last line

and **file2** contains

    this is line 1
    this is it
    line 3 of the file
    this line is very long

the command line

```
diff -s file1 file2
```

will display the following on the screen:

    file1: 5: line 5 of the file
    file1: 6: six six six six
    file1: 7: this is line 7
    file1: 8: line 8
    file1: 9: last line

```
/*
 * NAME: diff.c
 *
 * FUNCTION: Compares two files and displays the lines and line
 *           numbers of the lines which differ.
 *
 * ROUTINES CALLED: writeln(); writes a line to stdout insuring that
 *                            only one newline character is written.
 *                  read_char(); reads a character from stdin and
 *                            destroys the input buffer.
 *
```

```
*                    str_index(); returns the starting location of a
*                           substring within a string.
*                    str_equal(); returns TRUE if two strings are equal,
*                           otherwise FALSE is returned.
*
* MACROS USED: NOT(); performs a Boolean NOT.
*
* VARIABLES USED: file1, file2: pointers to the files to compare.
*                 line_count: contains the current line number.
*                 lines_displayed: contains the number of lines
*                        that have been displayed.
*                 file1_index: index into argv[] of the name of
*                        file1.
*                 file2_indes: index into argv[] of the name of
*                        file2.
*                 stop_scrolling: TRUE if scrolling is suppressed.
*                 eof_1: TRUE if the end of file1 has occurred.
*                 eof_2: TRUE if the end of file2 has occurred.
*                 done_with_file_comparison: TRUE or FALSE.
*                 string1: line read from file1.
*                 string2: line read from file2.
*                 argv: array of pointers to the command line.
*                 argc: number of command line arguments.
*
* PSEUDO CODE: if (enough command line arguments are not present)
*                  print an error message
*                  exit to the operating system
*
*              if (the value in argc == 4)  -- diff -s file1 file2
*                  if (if qualifier is not valid)
*                     print an error message
*                     do not suppress scrolling
*                  else
*                     suppress scrolling
*
*              if (the input and output file names are the same)
*                  print "files are identical"
*                  exit to the operating system
*
*              if (either of the files cannot be opened)
*                  print an error message
*                  exit to the operating system
*
*              initialize line_count to 0
*              initialize lines_displayed to 0
*
*              while (NOT done_with_file_comparison)
*                  if (the end of file1 has not occurred)
*                  get a line from file1
*
*                  if (the end of file2 has not occurred)
*                  get a line from file2
*
*                  if (one file has reached the end of file)
*                     display the line_count, and line the read
*                       from the other file since it is different
*                     increment the lines_displayed
*
```

```
*                   else if (both files have reached the end of file)
*                       set done_with_file_comparison to TRUE
*
*                   else if (the strings are not equal)
*                       print the line_count and both strings
*                       increment lines_displayed
*
*               if (suppress scrolling is desired)
*                   if (a screenful of lines has been written)
*                       prompt the user to hit <RETURN>
*                       set lines_displayed to 0
*
*               increment line_count
*
*           close the files
*
*/

#include <stdio.h>      /* contains definitions for file I/O */
#include "defn.h"
#include "math.h"
#include "strings.h"
#include "writeln.c"  /* contains the routine writeln() */
#include "readchar.c" /* contains the routine readchar() */
#include "strindex.c" /* contains the routine str_index() */
#include "strequal.c" /* contains the routine strings_are_equal() */

#define DISPLAY_PAGE 20   /* number of lines to display before
                             pausing for the user to hit <return> */

main (argc, argv)
  int argc;               /* number of command line arguments */
  char *argv[];           /* array of pointers to the command line */
  {
  FILE *file1;            /* first file specified in command line */
  FILE *file2;            /* second file specified in command line */
  FILE *fopen ();

  int line_count;           /* line number we are displaying */
  int lines_displayed = 0; /* number of lines we've displayed */
                            /* on this screenful */

  int file1_index = argc - 2; /* location in the array argv[] of the
                                 name of the file for file1 */
  int file2_index = argc - 1; /* location in the array argv[] of the
                                 name of the file for file2 */

  int stop_scrolling = FALSE;  /* TRUE if the -s qualifier is present */

  int eof_1 = FALSE;      /* end of file 1 */
  int eof_2 = FALSE;      /* end of file 2 */

  int done_with_file_comparison = FALSE;

  char string1[MAX_STRING]; /* line read from file1 */
  char string2[MAX_STRING]; /* line read from file2 */
```

```
if (argc < 3)         /* see if the file names are present */
  {
   printf ("diff: invalid useage: diff [-s] file1 file2\n");
   exit (1);
  }


/* see if the qualifier -s was provided to suppress scrolling */

if (argc == 4)   /* diff -x file file */
 {
  if (str_index ("-S-s", argv[1]) == -1)
    {
     printf ("diff: invalid qualifier %s use -s\n", argv[1]);
     printf ("diff: scrolling will not be suppressed\n");
     printf ("diff: hit <return> to continue\n");
     read_char ();
    }

  else
    stop_scrolling = TRUE;   /* user wants scrolling suppressed */
 }

/* see if the user is trying to open the same file twice */

if (strings_are_equal (argv[file1_index], argv[file2_index]))
  {
   printf ("diff: files are identical\n");
   exit (0);
  }

/* see if the files were successfully opened and, if so, display
 * the differences, otherwise print an error message.
 */

if ((file1 = fopen (argv[file1_index], "r")) == NULL)

  {
   printf ("diff: error opening the file %s\n", argv[file1_index]);
   exit (1);
  }

if ((file2 = fopen (argv[file2_index], "r")) == NULL)
  {
   printf ("diff: error opening file %s\n", argv[file2_index]);
   exit (1);
  }

/* find and display any differences along with the line number */

for (line_count = 1; NOT(done_with_file_comparison); line_count++)
  {
   /* test for the end of file 1 */

   if (NOT(eof_1))
     if (fgets (string1, MAX_STRING, file1) == NULL)
        eof_1 = TRUE;
```

```
/* test for the end of file 2 */

if (NOT(eof_2))
  if (fgets (string2, MAX_STRING, file2) == NULL)
    eof_2 = TRUE;

if (NOT(eof_1) && NOT(eof_2))  /* compare the strings */
 {
  if (strings_are_equal (string1, string2) == FALSE)
    {
      printf ("\n%s: %d: ", argv[file1_index], line_count);
      writeln (string1);

      printf ("%s: %d: ", argv[file2_index], line_count);
      writeln (string2);

      lines_displayed +=3;  /* for the display page count */
    }
 }

else if (NOT(eof_1))
  {
      printf ("\n%s: %d: ", argv[file1_index], line_count);
      writeln (string1);
      lines_displayed++;
  }

else if (NOT(eof_2))
  {
      printf ("\n%s: %d: ", argv[file2_index], line_count);
      writeln (string2);
      lines_displayed++;
  }
      else
        done_with_file_comparison = TRUE;


/* if the user has entered the stop_scroll qualifier (-s), we want
 * to stop the output after each page is displayed.  since the number
 * of lines displayed gets incremented by 3 in one instance and 1 in
 * others, the mod operator (%) will not work (i.e. lines_diplayed % 20)
 * For example,
 * if seven lines in a row are different, lines_displayed will equal 21
 * so the test lines_displayed % 20 fails and the output will continue
 * to scroll.  therefore, we will keep a count of the number of lines
 * we have displayed on this page.  once this count is > DISPLAY_PAGE
 * we will prompt the user for a return and reset the count for the next
 * page.
 */

      if (lines_displayed > DISPLAY_PAGE && stop_scrolling)
        {
          printf ("\nHit <RETURN> to continue\n");

          read_char();

          lines_displayed = 0;
```

```
      }
   }

 fclose (file1);
 fclose (file2);
}
```

The Findword program finds and displays each line containing the word specified in the command line. This program is similar to the UNIX utility **grep**. The calling sequence for Findword is

```
findword [-stop scrolling] word file
```

The optional qualifier -s again suppresses scrolling once a screenful of information has been written. If **file1** contains

this is line 1
this is it
line 3 of the file
this line is very long
line 5 of the file
six six six six
this is line 7
line 8
last line

the command line

```
findword -s is file1
```

will display the following on the screen:

file1: 1: this is line 1
file1: 2: this is it
file1: 4: this line is very long
file1: 7: this is line 7

The output of Findword may be redirected to **file1** as in the previous programs.

```
findword -s is file1 > outfile
```

```
/*
 * NAME: findword.c
 *
 * FUNCTION: Displays the contents and line number of all lines in
 *           the file which contain the word specified in the
 *           command line.
 *
 * ROUTINES CALLED: writeln(); writes a line to the stdout insuring
 *                            only one newline character is written.
 *                  read_char(); reads a character from stdin and
 *                             destroys the contents of the input
 *                             buffer.
 *                  str_index(); returns the starting location of
 *                             a substring within a string, or -1
 *                             if the substring did not exist.
 *
 * VARIABLES USED: input_file: pointer to the input file.
 *                 line_number: current line number.
 *                 lines_displayed: number of lines displayed.
 *                 stop_scrolling: if TRUE, scrolling is suppressed,
 *                             otherwise lines will continue to
 *                             scoll.
 *                 word_index: index into argv[] containing
 *                             the word to find.
 *                 file_index: index into argv[] containing
 *                             the name of the file to search
 *                             for the word.
 *
 *
 * PSEUDO CODE: if (enough command line arguments are not present)
 *                 print an error message (should be: findword word file)
 *                 exit to the operating system
 *
 *              if (argc == 4)
 *                 if (the qualifier is valid)
 *                    suppress scrolling
 *                 else
 *                    display an error message
 *                    do not suppress scrolling
 *
 *              if (the file cannot be opened)
 *                 display an error message
 *                 exit to the operating system
 *
 *              initialize the line number to 0
 *
 *              while (the file contains lines)
 *                 get a line from the file
 *                 increment the line number
 *                 if (the line contains the word)
 *                    print the line number and line
 *                    increment the count of lines displayed
 *
 *                 if (scrolling supression is desired)
 *                    if (a page has been displayed)
 *                       pause and prompt for <RETURN>
 *                       set lines displayed to 0
 *
```

```
*                      increment the line number
*
*                   close the file
*
*/

#include <stdio.h>       /* contains definitions for file I/O */
#include "defn.h"
#include "strings.h"
#include "writeln.c"  /* contains the routine writeln() */
#include "readchar.c" /* contains the routine readchar() */
#include "strindex.c" /* contains the routine str_index() */

#define DISPLAY_PAGE 20 /* number of lines to display before
                            pausing if scrolling has been supressed */

main (argc, argv)
  int argc;             /* number of command line arguments */
  char *argv[];         /* array of pointers to the command line */
{
  FILE *input_file;  /* file to search for the word specified */
  FILE *fopen ();

  int line_number = 0;          /* line number we are displaying */

  int lines_displayed = 0;      /* number of lines we have displayed */
                                /* on the current page */

  int stop_scrolling = FALSE; /* TRUE if user wants to suppress
                                 scrolling with each page */

  int word_index = argc - 2;  /* location of the word in argv[] */
  int file_index = argc - 1;  /* location of the file name in argv[] */

  char string[MAX_STRING];    /* line read from the file */

  if (argc < 3)               /* see if the file name is present */
  {
    printf ("findword: invalid useage: findword [-s] word file\n");
    exit (1);
  }

  if (argc == 4) /* see if the qualifier is valid */
  {
    if (str_index ("-s-S", argv[1]) == -1)
    {
      printf ("findword: invalid qualifier %s use -s\n", argv[1]);
      printf ("scrolling will not be suppressed\n");
      printf ("Hit <RETURN> to continue\n");
      read_char ();
    }
    else
      stop_scrolling = TRUE;
  }

  /* see if the file was successfully opened and, if so, display
   * the lines containing the word, otherwise print an error message.
   */
```

```
if ((input_file = fopen (argv[file_index], "r")) == NULL)
 {
  printf ("findword: error opening file %s\n", argv[file_index]);
  exit (1);
 }

/* find and display each occurrence of the word */

while (fgets (string, MAX_STRING, input_file))
  {
   line_number++;

/* if the line contains the word, print the line
   number and the contents of the string */

   if (str_index (string, argv[word_index]) != -1)
     {
       printf ("\n%s: %d:", argv[file_index], line_number);
       writeln (string);
       lines_displayed += 2;  /* \n and string */
     }

   /* see if scrolling should be suppressed */

   if (lines_displayed > DISPLAY_PAGE  && stop_scrolling)
     {
       printf ("\nHit <RETURN> to continue\n");

       read_char();

       lines_displayed = 0;
     }
  }

 fclose (input_file);
}
```

The Replace program replaces or deletes every occurrence of a word within a file. The calling sequence for Replace is

```
replace [qualifier] word [word] file [output_file]
```

The qualifiers supported by Replace are

-d   directs the program to delete each occurrence of the word.

-r   directs the program to replace each occurrence of the word with the second word specified in the command line.

If **file1** contains

this is line 1
this is it
line 3 of the file
this line is very long
line 5 of the file
six six six six
this is line 7
line 8
last line

the command line

```
replace -r six 6 file1
```

will display the following on the screen:

this is line 1
this is it
line 3 of the file
this line is very long
line 5 of the file
6 6 6 6
this is line 7
line 8
last line

To delete each occurrence of the word "this" and write the new file to **newfile.dat**, enter the command

```
replace -d this file1 newfile.dat
```

```
/*
 * NAME: replace.c
 *
 * FUNCTION: Deletes or replaces each occurrence of a word within
 *           a file.
 *
 * ROUTINES CALLED: str_index(); returns the starting location of
 *                            a substring within a string.
 *                  remove_substring(); removes a substring from
 *                                    a string.
 *
```

```
*                      insert_string(); inserts a substring into a
*                                       string at the location specified.
*                      strings_are_equal(); returns TRUE if two strings
*                                       are equal, otherwise FALSE is
*                                       returned.
*
* VARIABLES USED: delete: TRUE if the word is to be deleted.
*                 replace: TRUE if the word is to be replaced.
*                 input_index: location of the name of the input
*                              file in the array argv[].
*                 output_index: location of the name of the output
*                               file in the array argv[].
*                 input_file: pointer to input file.
*                 output_file: pointer to output file.
*                 location: location of the substring in the string.
*                 length: length of the substring.
*                 string: line read from the file.
*                 argc: number of command line arguments.
*                 argv: array of pointers to the command line.
*
* PSEUDO CODE: if (enough command line arguments are not present)
*                 print an error message
*                 exit to the operating system
*
*              find out which qualifier was provided -d or -r
*
*              if (the qualifier == -r)
*                increment input_index to point to the name of
*                  the input file in the array argv[]
*                increment output_index to point to the name of
*                  the output file in the array argv[]
*                set replace to TRUE
*
*          --  command line will contain the
*              following if the qualifier is -r
*
*              replace -r word new_word file [file]
*
*              else if (the qualifier = -d)
*                set delete to TRUE
*
*              if (the qualifier is invalid)
*                print an error message
*                exit to the operating system
*
*              if (the input and output files are the same)
*                print an error message
*                exit to the operating system -- most micro computer
*                  operating systems will not allow us to open the
*                  the same file twice
*
*              if (either of the files cannot be opened)
*                print an error message
*                exit to the operating system
*
*              if (no output file is specified)
*                output_file = stdout
*
```

```
*              get the length of the substring
*
*              while (the input file contains lines)
*                  get a line from the input file
*                  while (the line contains the substring)
*                      if (delete)
*                          remove the substring
*                      else
*                          remove the substring
*                          insert the new string
*
*
*              close the file(s)
*
*/

#include <stdio.h>      /* contains definitions for file I/O */
#include "defn.h"
#include "strings.h"
#include "strindex.c" /* contains the routine str_index() */
#include "strlen.c"   /* contains the routine string_length() */
#include "strremss.c" /* contains the routine remove_substring() */
#include "strinsrt.c" /* contains the routine insert_string() */
#include "strcopy.c"  /* contains the routine string_copy() */
#include "strequal.c" /* contains the routine strings_are_equal() */

main (argc, argv)
  int argc;             /* number of command line arguments */
  char *argv[];         /* array of pointers to the command line */
{
  FILE *fopen(), *input_file, *output_file;

  int delete = FALSE;   /* TRUE if the user wants the word deleted */
  int replace = FALSE;  /* TRUE if the user wants the word replaced */

  int input_index = 3;  /* location in argv[] of the file names */
  int output_index = 4;

  int location;             /* location of the substring in the string */
  int length;               /* length of the substring */

  char string[MAX_STRING]; /* string read from the file */

  /* see if enough command line arguments are present */

  if (argc < 4)
   {
    printf ("replace error: replace -dr word [word] file [file]\n");
    exit (1);
   }

  /* see which qualifier is present (-d) delete or (-r) replace */

  if (str_index("-d-D", argv[1]) != -1)
   delete = TRUE;

  else if (str_index ("-r-R", argv[1]) != -1)
   {
```

```
      replace = TRUE;
      input_index++;      /* location in argv[] of file names */
      output_index++;     /* + 1 due to replacement word     */
   }

/* if the user wants to replace the substring with another string
 * the replacement string will be in the command line prior to the
 * names of the input and output file names.  we must therefore,
 * increment input_index and output_index to the file names.
 */

else
  {
   printf ("replace: error in qualifier use -d or -r\n");
   exit(1);
  }

  /* make sure that the output file name is different
     from the input file */

  if (strings_are_equal (argv[input_index], argv[output_index]))
    {
     printf ("replace: input file must differ from output file\n");
     exit(1);
    }

/* see if the the input file is specified */

if (argc < 5 && replace)
  {
   printf ("replace error: replace -dq word [word] file [file]\n");
   exit (1);
  }

/* see if the input file can be opened */

else if ((input_file = fopen (argv[input_index], "r")) == NULL)
  {
   printf ("replace: error opening file %s\n", argv[input_index]);
   exit(1);
  }

/* see if an output file is desired, or if the output
   should go to the standard output via stdout */

if (delete && argc == 4)          /* remove -d word filename */
   output_file = stdout;

else if (replace && argc == 5)  /* remove -r word word filename */
   output_file = stdout;

else if ((output_file = fopen (argv[output_index], "w")) == NULL)
    {
     printf ("replace: error opening file %s\n", argv[output_index]);
     exit(1);
    }

/* get the length of the old string */
```

```
  length = string_length (argv[2]);

  /* update the file */

  while (fgets (string, MAX_STRING, input_file))
    {

    /* while the string contains the substring, delete or
       replace it */

      while ((location = str_index (string, argv[2])) != -1)

        if (delete)
          remove_substring (string, location, length);

        else
          {
          /* remove the string we are replacing */
          remove_substring (string, location, length);

          /* insert the new string */
          insert_string (string, argv[3], location);
          }

      fputs (string, output_file); /* write the corrected string */
    }

  fclose (input_file);
}
```

The program Crypt encrypts a file to protect it from other users. The calling sequence for Crypt is

```
crypt key file [output_file]
```

The **key** is your encryption key. Once a file is encrypted, the same key must be used to decrypt it. For example, to encrypt a file, use

```
crypt ;:.,? file1 file
```

To decrypt it use the same key.

```
crypt ;:.,? file file1
```

```
/*
 * NAME: crypt.c
 *
 * FUNCTION: Encrypts or decrypts a file with the key passed to
 *           it in the command line.
 *
 * ROUTINES CALLED: strings_are_equal(); returns TRUE if two strings
 *                                       are equal, otherwise FALSE
 *                                       is returned.
```

```
*                   crypt(): encrypts or decrypts the file it receives
*                           based upon the key provided.
*
* VARIABLES USED: input_file: pointer to the input file.
*                 output_file: pointer to the output file.
*                 argv: array of pointers to the command line.
*                 argc: number of command line arguments.
*
* PSEUDO CODE: if (enough command line arguments are not present)
*                 print an error message
*                 exit to the operating system
*
*              if (the input and output files are the same)
*                 print an error message
*                 exit to the operating system -- most micro
*                    computer operating systems will not allow
*                    us to open the same file twice
*
*              if (either the input or output file cannot be opened)
*                 print an error message
*                 exit to the operating system
*
*              invoke crypt() to encrypt the file
*
*              close the file(s)
*
*/

#include <stdio.h>       /* contains definitions for file I/O */
#include "defn.h"
#include "math.h"
#include "strings.h"
#include "fwriteln.c" /* contains the routine fwriteln() */
#include "strlen.c"   /* contains the routine string_length() */
#include "strequal.c" /* contains the routine strings_are_equal() */

main (argc, argv)
  int argc;              /* number of command line arguments */
  char *argv[];          /* array of pointers to the command line */
 {
  FILE *input_file;
  FILE *output_file;
  FILE *fopen ();

if (argc < 3)        /* see if the input file name is present */
 {
  printf ("crypt: invalid useage: crypt key file [file]\n");
  exit (1);
 }

/* make sure that the input and output files are different */

if (strings_are_equal (argv[2], argv[3]))
 {
   printf ("crypt: input and output file must differ\n");
   exit (1);
 }
```

```
/* see if the file was successfully opened and, if so,
 * invoke the routine crypt() to encrypt or decrypt the
 * lines it contains, otherwise print an error message.
 */

if ((input_file = fopen (argv[2], "r")) == NULL)
  {
  printf ("crypt: error opening file %s\n", argv[2]);
  exit (1);
  }

if (argc < 4)              /* crypt key file */
  output_file = stdout;    /* no output file was specified */
else
  if ((output_file = fopen (argv[3], "w")) == NULL)
    {
    printf ("crypt: error opening file %s\n", argv[3]);
    exit (1);
    }

crypt (input_file, output_file, argv[1]);

fclose (input_file);

if (argc == 4)              /* if the output was directed to stdout */
  fclose (output_file); /* don't close a file */
}




/*
 * NAME: crypt (input_file, output_file, key)
 *
 * FUNCTION: Encrypts a previously unencrypted file with the key
 *           specified, or decrypts a file encrypted with the key
 *           provided, and writes the new data to the file pointed
 *           to by output_file.
 *
 * EXAMPLE: crypt (argv[1], argv[2], argv[3]);
 *
 * VARIABLES USED: input_file: pointer to the input file.
 *                 output_file: pointer to the output file.
 *                 key: key used for encryption/decryption.
 *                 key_length: number of characters in the key.
 *                 letter: letter read from the file.
 *
 * ROUTINES CALLED: string_length(); returns the length of a string.
 *
 * PSEUDO CODE: get the length of the key
 *              while (the file contains data)
 *                  get a character from the file
 *                  if (the character is not a control character)
 *                      encrypt the character
 *
```

```
*                    if (the new character is a control character)
*                      encrypt the character back to its original value
*
*                 write the character to the output file
*
*/
crypt (input_file, output_file, key)
  FILE *input_file;
  FILE *output_file;
  char key[];            /* key to use in the encryption/decryption */
{
  int letter;            /* buffer for letter read from the file */

  int key_length;        /* number of characters in the key */

  int i = 0;

  key_length = string_length (key);  /* get the length of the key */

    while ((letter = getc(input_file)) != -1)
      {
       if (NOT(is_control(letter)))
         {
          letter = XOR(letter, key[i %  key_length]);

/* we will test to insure the result of the XOR is not a control
   character. if it is, we will convert it back to the original
   character. this is because a control z represents an end of
   file. if we write this value, the program which decrypts the
   file will think it has found the end of file due to the control
   z.  since control characters do not appear often in a file,
   converting the character back to its original value
   does not affect the encrypted result. likewise, when we later
   decrypt the file, the correct letter is obtained since it is
   first converted to a control character, and then back to its
   original value.
*/
          if (is_control(letter))
            letter = XOR(letter, key[i %  key_length]);

          putc(letter, output_file);

          i++;
        }
      else
        putc(letter, output_file);
    }
 }



/* the characters are encrypted as follows:

        key = mykey
```

```
string = this is it

keylength = 5

XOR(t,m);
XOR(h,y);
XOR(i,k);
XOR(s,e);
XOR( ,y);
XOR(i,m);
XOR(s,y);
XOR( ,k);
XOR(i,e);
XOR(s,y);
```

```
*/
```

The **#include** statement has been used with many of the programs in this chapter to include routines that are contained in other source files. As you may recall, the **#include** statement simplifies your programming task by allowing you to reference the file containing the desired routine, instead of having to copy the file into your source file. Including the additional code often adds to the programmer's confusion, since ease of understanding is often inversely related to the number of lines of code contained in a routine. However, eliminating the code for the routine may also confuse individuals who are unfamiliar with the routine being included. For this reason, most experienced programmers discourage the use of the **#include** statement. The following Include program allows a programmer to develop a routine by including routines contained in other files, and later, to replace each **#include** statement with the actual contents of the file being included.

The following command invokes the program:

```
include file_name [output_file_name]
```

The routine will open the file specified in the command line and invoke the routine **write＿define( )**, which will examine the file for **#include** statements. If a file is included, the routine will open the file to be included and recursively invoke itself to examine the contents of the new file for **#include** statements. If a file to be included cannot be opened, the routine will leave the **#include** statement and to its right insert a comment stating that the file could not be opened.

```
/*
 * NAME: include.c
 *
 * FUNCTION: Examines a file for #include statements and replaces the
 *           statement with the contents of the file that is being
 *           included. This increases the readability of the source
 *           file by providing the reader with the actual code for each
 *           routine referenced.
 *
 * VARIABLES USED: input_file: pointer to the file to examine for
 *                             #include statements.
 *                 output_file: pointer to the output file or stdout.
 *
 * ROUTINE CALLED: write_include(): examines the file it receives for
 *                                  #include statements and replaces the
 *                                  file being included with its
 *                                  actual contents.
 *
 * PSEUDO CODE: if (enough command line arguments are not present)
 *                  print an error message
 *                  exit to the operating system
 *
 *              if (the input and output files are the same)
 *                  print an error message
 *                  exit to the operating system -- most micro computer
 *                    operating systems will not allow to open the same
 *                    file twice
 *
 *              if (either of the files cannot be opened)
 *                  print an error message
 *                  exit to the operating system
 *
 *              invoke the routine write_include() to write the contents
 *                of the input file along with any files which are
 *                #included to the output file
 *
 *              close the file(s)
 *
 */

#include <stdio.h>
#include "defn.h"
#include "strings.h"
#include "strcopy.c"      /* contains the routine copy_string() */
#include "strremss.c"     /* contains the routine remove_substring() */
#include "strindex.c"     /* contains the routine str_index() */
#include "ptrrepc.c"      /* contains the routine replace_character() */
#include "strcidex.c"     /* contains the routine char_index() */
#include "strlen.c"       /* contains the routine string_length() */
#include "strremb.c"      /* contains the routine remove_blanks() */
#include "strequal.c"     /* contains the routine strings_are_equal() */

main (argc, argv)
  int argc;               /* count of command line arguments */
  char *argv[];           /* array of pointers to the command line */
  {
  FILE *input_file, *output_file, *fopen();
```

```
  if (argc < 2)
   {
    printf ("include: invalid useage: include file_name [file_name]\n");
    exit(1);
   }

  if (strings_are_equal (argv[1], argv[2]))
   {
    printf ("include: input file must differ from output file\n");
    exit (1);
   }

  else if ((input_file = fopen (argv[1], "r")) == NULL)
   {
    printf ("include: error opening %s for input\n", argv[1]);
    exit(1);
   }

  if (argc == 2)   /* no output file was specified */
   output_file = stdout;

  else if ((output_file = fopen (argv[2], "w")) == NULL)
   {
    printf ("include: error opening %s for output\n", argv[2]);
    exit(1);
   }

  write_include (input_file, output_file);

  fclose (input_file);

  if (argc > 2) /* an output file was opened */
   fclose (output_file);
 }

/*
 * NAME: write_include (input_file, output_file);
 *
 * FUNCTION: Writes the contents of the file it receives while searching
 *           for #include statements.  If an #include statement is found,
 *           write_include() invokes itself recursively to write the
 *           contents of the file being included while examining it for
 *           additional #include statements.
 *
 * VARIABLES USED: input_file: file pointer to the file to examine for
 *                             #include statements.
 *                 output_file: destination of the output (file or stdout).
 *                 new_file: file pointer to a file being #included.
 *                 string: line read from the file.
 *
 *                 file_name: string containing the file name of a file
 *                            which is being #included.
 *                 location: location of the substring containing #include
 *                           within the line read from the file.
 *                 char_location: character location of the quotes or
 *                            brackets which surround a file name
 *                            which is being #included.
 *
```

```
 * ROUTINES CALLED: str_index(): returns the starting location of a
 *                               substring within a string, or -1 if
 *                               substring is not found.
 *                  copy_string(): copies the contents of the first
 *                               string to the second.
 *                  remove_substring(): removes the substring specified
 *                               from a string.
 *                  char_index: returns the character location of the first
 *                               occurrence of a character within a string,
 *                               or -1 if the character is not found.
 *
 * PSEUDO CODE: while (the input file contains lines)
 *                 get a line from the file
 *                 if (a file is being #included)
 *                   if (the file can be opened)
 *                     invoke write_include() to include the file
 *                   else
 *                     leave the #include statement and include the
 *                         comment -- "could not open the file"
 *                 else
 *                   write the line to the output file
 *
 *              return
 *
 */

write_include (input_file, output_file)
  FILE *output_file, *input_file;
{
  FILE *fopen(), *new_file;

  char string[MAX_STRING];      /* string read from the file */
  char file_name[MAX_STRING];   /* file name of the new file */

  int location;                 /* location of the substring
                                   #include in the string read */
  int char_location;

  while (fgets (string, MAX_STRING, input_file))

  /* see if a file is being #included */

  if ((location = str_index (string, "#include")) != -1)
    {
      if (location != 0)    /* #include must begin in the first column */
        fputs (string, output_file);

    else   /* get the file name of the file being #included */
      {
        copy_string (string, file_name);

        remove_substring (file_name, 0, 8); /* remove #include */

        if ((char_location = char_index (file_name, '"')) != -1)
          {
            remove_substring (file_name, char_location, 1);
            replace_character (file_name, '"', NULL);
          }
```

```
  else
  {
     /* check for the brackets <> in the include statement */

     if ((char_location = char_index (file_name, '<')) != -1)
       remove_substring (file_name, char_location, 1);
     if ((char_location = char_index (file_name, '>')) != -1)
       remove_substring (file_name, char_location, 1);

     file_name[char_location] = NULL;
  }

  remove_blanks (file_name);

  /* see if the file can be opened */

  if ((new_file =  fopen (file_name, "r")) ==  NULL)
  {
    fprintf (output_file, "%s", string);
    fprintf (output_file, "/* could not open the file %s */\n",
             file_name);
  }
  else  /* invoke write_include() recursively to examine */
  {    /* the file which is being #included */
    write_include (new_file, output_file);
    fclose (new_file);
  }
 }
 }
else
  fputs (string, output_file);
}
```

The Linecnt program returns a count of the number of lines contained in a file. The calling sequence for Linecnt is

```
linecnt file
```

If the file passed to Linecnt contains

this is line 1
this is it
line 3 of the file
this line is very long
line 5 of the file
six six six six
this is line 7
line 8
last line

the output of Linecnt is: The number of lines in the file is 9.

```
/*
 * NAME: linecnt.c
 *
 * FUNCTION: Prints the number of lines contained in a file.
 *
 * ROUTINES CALLED: file_line_count(); returns the number of lines
 *                                     in a file, or -1 if the file
 *                                     cannot be opened.
 *
 * VARIABLES USED: num_lines: number of lines in the file.
 *                 argv: array of pointers to the command line.
 *                 argc: number of command line arguments.
 *
 * PSEUDO CODE: if (enough command line arguments are not present)
 *                  print an error message
 *                  exit to the operating system
 *
 *              get the number of lines in the file from the
 *                  routine file_line_count()
 *
 *              if (-1 was returned from the routine file_line_count())
 *                  print "the file could not be opened"
 *
 *              else (the file was successfully opened)
 *                  print the number of lines in the file
 *
 */

#include <stdio.h>          /* definitions required for file I/O */
#include "defn.h"
#include "filelen.c"         /* contains the routine file_line_count() */

main (argc, argv)
  int argc;                  /* number of command line arguments */
  char *argv[];              /* array of pointers to the command line */
{
  int num_lines;             /* the number of lines in the file */

  if (argc < 2)              /* see if the file name is present */
  {
    printf ("linecnt: no file specified\n");
    exit (1);
  }

  /* see if the file was successfully opened and, if so, print
   * the number of lines it contained, otherwise print an error
   * message.
   */

  if ((num_lines = file_line_count (argv[1])) != ERROR)
    printf ("The number of lines in %s is %d\n", argv[1], num_lines);

    else
      printf ("linecnt: error opening file %s\n", argv[1]);
  }
```

```
/*
 * NAME: file_line_count (file_name)
 *
 * FUNCTION: Returns the number of lines in a file.
 *
 * EXAMPLE: length_of_file = file_line_count (argv[3]);
 *
 * VARIABLES USED: file_pointer: pointer to the file to be examined.
 *                 line_count: number of lines in the file.
 *
 *
 * PSEUDO CODE: if (the file cannot be opened)
 *                  return (-1)
 *
 *              else
 *                  initialize the count of lines to 0
 *                  while (the file contains lines)
 *                      get a line from the file
 *                      increment the count of lines
 *
 *                  close the file
 *
 *                  return (the count of the number of lines)
 *
 */
file_line_count (file_name)
  char *file_name;
 {
  int line_count = -1;      /* number of lines in the file */

  char buffer[MAX_STRING]; /* string read from the file */

  FILE *file_pointer;

  /* see if the file can be opened, else return the value -1 */

  if ((file_pointer = fopen (file_name, "r")) != NULL)
   {
    for (line_count = 0; fgets (buffer, MAX_STRING, file_pointer);
                                                   line_count++)
      ;
    fclose (file_pointer);
   }

  return (line_count); /* number of lines in the file */
 }
```

The Show program displays a file to the terminal a screenful at a time rather than allowing the output to scroll until the user hits a scroll lock. This routine is similar to the UNIX command **more**. In addition, Show will display the percentage of the file that has been displayed on the screen. The calling sequence for Show is

```
show filename
```

```
/*
 * NAME: show.c
 *
 * FUNCTION: Displays the contents of a file to the screen one
 *           screenful at a time.  In addition, the routine
 *           displays the percentage of the file which has been
 *           displayed.
 *
 * ROUTINES CALLED: writeln(): writes a string to stdout insuring
 *                             that only one newline character is
 *                             written.
 *                  readchar(): reads a character and destroys the
 *                              contents of the input buffer.
 *                  file_line_count(): returns the number of lines
 *                                     in a file.
 *
 * VARIABLES USED: input_file: file to display.
 *                 line_count: number of lines displayed.
 *                 percent_shown: percentage of the file that
 *                                has been displayed.
 *                 length_of_file: number of lines in the input file.
 *                 argc: number of command line arguments.
 *                 argv: array of pointers to the command line.
 *                 string: line read from the file.
 *
 * PSEUDO CODE: if (enough command line arguments are not present)
 *                  print an error message
 *                  exit to the operating system
 *
 *              get the length of the file
 *              if (the length is -1)
 *                print "file could not be opened"
 *                exit to the operating system
 *
 *              if (the file cannot be reopened for reading)
 *                  print "file could not be opened"
 *                  exit to the operating system
 *
 *              initialize the line count to 0
 *              while (lines are in the input file)
 *                  get a line from the file
 *                  display the line to stdout
 *                  increment the line count
 *
 *                  if (a screenful has been displayed)
 *                    print the percentage of the file that
 *                        has been displayed
 *                    pause and prompt the user to hit <RETURN>
 *
 *              close the file
 */


#include <stdio.h>      /* contains definitions for file I/O */
#include "defn.h"
#include "strings.h"
#include "math.h"
```

```
#include "writeln.c"  /* contains the routine writeln() */
#include "readchar.c" /* contains the routine readchar() */
#include "filelen.c"  /* contains the routine file_line_count() */

#define DISPLAY_PAGE 20  /* number of lines to display before
                            pausing with the display message */

main (argc, argv)
  int argc;            /* number of command line arguments */
  char *argv[];        /* array of pointers to the command line entered */
{
  FILE *input_file; /* file to show on the screen */
  FILE *fopen ();

  int line_count = 0; /* line number we are displaying */
  int length_of_file; /* number of lines in the file */
  int percent_shown;  /* percentage of the file that has been displayed */

  char string[MAX_STRING]; /* line read from the file */

  if (argc < 2)             /* see if the file name is present */
  {
    printf ("show: no file specified\n");
    exit (1);
  }

/* find out how many lines are in the file to be displayed.
   if the file cannot be opened, the value -1 is returned,
   so display an error message and exit to the operating system. */

  if ((length_of_file = file_line_count (argv[1])) == ERROR)
    {
      printf ("show: error opening the file %s\n", argv[1]);
      exit (1);
    }

  /* reopen the file for display */

  if ((input_file = fopen (argv[1], "r")) == NULL)
  {
    printf ("show: error opening file %s\n", argv[1]);
    exit (1);
  }

  /* read a line from the file and display it.
     once the number of lines displayed is equal to the
     display page, pause displaying the percentage of the file
     that has been displayed, and ask the user to hit <RETURN>. */

  while (fgets (string, MAX_STRING, input_file))
    {
      writeln (string);  /* display the line */

    if (++line_count % DISPLAY_PAGE == 0)
      {
        printf ("\n\nPercentage of file displayed %d\n",
          (int) percent(line_count, length_of_file));
```

```
        printf ("Hit <RETURN> to continue\n");

        read_char(); /* read the carriage return and empty
                         the input buffer. */
      }
   }

 fclose (input_file);
}
```

The Wordcnt program provides a quick summary of the number of lines, words, characters, and pages (66 lines per page) contained in a file. This routine is similar to the UNIX command **wc**. If the file contains the following,

> this is line 1
> this is it
> line 3 of the file
> this line is very long
> line 5 of the file
> six six six six
> this is line 7
> line 8
> last line

the output of Wordcnt b:test is

> file: b: test
> page count: 0
> line count: 9
> word count: 34
> character count: 126

The calling sequence for Wordcnt is

```
    wordcnt file_name
```

```
/*
 * NAME: wordcnt.c
 *
 * FUNCTION: Displays the number of lines, words, characters, and
 *           pages (66 lines / page) in a file.
 *
```

```
 * ROUTINES USED: wordcnt_file(); returns the number of lines, words
 *                and characters in a file.
 *
 * VARIABLES USED: input_file: pointer to the input file.
 *                 word_cnt: number of words in the file.
 *                 line_cnt: number of lines in the file.
 *                 char_cnt: number of characters in the file.
 *                 argc: number of command line arguments.
 *                 argv: array of pointers to the command line.
 *
 * PSEUDO CODE: if (enough command line arguments are not specified)
 *                 print an error message
 *                 exit to the operating system
 *
 *              if (the input file cannot be opened)
 *                 print "the file cannot be opened"
 *                 exit to the operating system
 *
 *              invoke the routine wordcnt_file() to count the
 *              number of characters, words, and lines in the
 *              file
 *
 *              print the number of pages, lines, words, and
 *              characters contained in the file
 *
 *              close the input_file
 *
 */

#include <stdio.h>        /* contains definitions for file I/0 */
#include "b:defn.h"
#include "b:strings.h"

main (argc, argv)
  int argc;               /* number of command line arguments */
  char *argv[];           /* array of pointers to the command
                             line entered */
{
  FILE *input_file;
  FILE *fopen ();

  int word_cnt;           /* number of words in the file */
  int line_cnt;           /* number of lines in the file */
  int char_cnt;           /* number of characters in the file */

  if (argc < 2)           /* see if file name is present */
{
  printf ("wordcnt: no file specified.\n");
  exit (1);
}

/* see if the file was successfully opened and, if so, count
 * the number of lines, words, and characters it contains and
 * print the totals, otherwise print an error message.
 */

if ((input_file = fopen (argv[1], "r")) == NULL)
{
```

```
      printf ("wordcnt: error opening file %s\n", argv[1]);
      exit (1);
   }

   wordcnt_file (input_file, &line_cnt, &word_cnt, &char_cnt);

   printf ("\nfile: %s\npage count: %d\nline count: %d\n",
            argv[1], line_cnt / 66, line_cnt);

   printf ("wordcnt: %d\ncharacter count: %d\n", word_cnt, char_cnt);

   fclose (input_file);
}




/*
 * NAME: wordcnt_file (input_file, line_cnt, word_cnt, char_cnt)
 *
 * FUNCTION: Returns a count of the number of lines, words, and
 *           characters contained in a file.
 *
 * VARIABLES USED: input_file: pointer to the input file.
 *                 line_cnt: number of lines in the file.
 *                 word_cnt: number of words in the file.
 *                 char_cnt: number of characters in the file.
 *                 string: line read from the file.
 *                 index: index into a character string.
 *                 series_of_blanks: Boolean value which states
 *                                   whether or not we are
 *                                   currently examining a series
 *                                   of blanks.
 *
 * MACROS USED: is_space(); returns TRUE if the character is a
 *                   blank, otherwise FALSE is returned.
 *
 * PSEUDO CODE: while (there are lines in the file)
 *                  get a line from the file
 *                  set series_of_blanks to TRUE
 *                  while (characters are in the string)
 *                    get a character
 *                    if (the character is a blank)
 *                      increment the character count
 *                      if (series_of_blanks is FALSE)
 *                          increment the word count
 *                          set series_of_blanks to TRUE
 *
 *                    else if (character is not end of line (EOL))
 *                        set series_of_blanks to FALSE
 *                        increment the character count
 *
 *                    if (series_of_blanks is FALSE)
 *                        increment the word count
 *
 *                    increment the line count
 *
 */
```

```
wordcnt_file (input_file, line_cnt, word_cnt, char_cnt)
 FILE *input_file;
 int *line_cnt;
 int *word_cnt;
 int *char_cnt;
{
 char string [MAX_STRING];   /* buffer for a line read
                                from the file */

 int index;
 int series_of_blanks;

/* we will increment the count of characters with each character read.
 * the line count is incremented with each NULL character or end of
 * line (\n) read.
 *
 * the word count is more difficult in that, a word is defined as a
 * sequence of characters separated by a blank.  For example,
 *
 *   this line has five words
 *
 * we also increment the word count on each NULL character.
 *
 * if the data has leading blanks, we will get an invalid word
 * count if we count each blank as a new word.  we will use the
 * variable series_of_blanks to tell us whether or not we are in a
 * series blanks. if so, we only will increment the character count
 * and not the word count.  once we find a character which is not
 * blank we will set series_of_blanks to FALSE to insure that the next
 * blank gets counted as an end of a word. the check to insure that
 * string[index] is not EOL when we reset series_of_blanks is to
 * prevent the carriage return linefeed from being interpreted as
 * as a word.
 *
 */

  *word_cnt = 0;
  *line_cnt = 0;
  *char_cnt = 0;

/* since we want to modify the values of several parameters in the
 * function, we have to use pointers to the variables.
 */

  while (fgets (string, MAX_STRING, input_file))
     {
       series_of_blanks = TRUE;

       for (index = 0; string[index] != NULL; index++)
        {
          if (is_blank(string[index]))
            {
             ++(*char_cnt);

             if (series_of_blanks == FALSE)
               {
```

```
                ++(*word_cnt);
                series_of_blanks = TRUE;
              }
          }

        else if (string[index] != EOL)
          {
            series_of_blanks = FALSE;
            ++(*char_cnt);
          }
      }

/* at this point we have an end of the line so we need to increment
 * the line count.
 *
 * we will also increment the word count as long as the line did not
 * end with a series of blanks.
 */

      if (series_of_blanks == FALSE)
          ++(*word_cnt);
      ++(*line_cnt);
    }
}
```

The Insert program inserts a file at the line specified in another file. The calling sequence for Insert is

```
insert line# file1 file2 [output_file]
```

For example, if **file1** contains

> this is line 1
> this is it
> line 3 of the file
> this line is very long
> line 5 of the file
> six six six six
> this is line 7
> line 8
> last line

and **file2** contains

new1
new2
new3

the command

insert 6 file1 file2

will display the following on the screen:

this is line 1
this is it
line 3 of the file
this line is very long
line 5 of the file
new1
new2
new3
six six six six
this is line 7
line 8
last line

If you want the output to be written to a file, you can use the redirection operator >, which redirects the output from **stdout** to the location specified:

```
insert 6 file1 file2 > output_file
```

As an alternative, you can provide the name of the desired output file within your command line:

```
insert 6 file1 file2 output_file
```

In this case, the Insert program will write the data to the file instead of the operating system. If you are using either UNIX or

MS-DOS, you can redirect the output of the remaining programs from the screen to the file you specify with the redirection operator (>).

```
/*
 * NAME: insert.c
 *
 * FUNCTION: Inserts a file into a second file at the line number
 *           specified in the command line.
 *
 * ROUTINES CALLED: int_convert(); converts a character string to
 *                                 an integer value.
 *                  file_line_count(); returns the number of lines
 *                                     in a file.
 *                  strings_are_equal(); returns TRUE if two strings
 *                                       are equal, otherwise FALSE
 *                                       is returned.
 *                  file_insert(); inserts a file into a second
 *                                 file at the line specified.
 *
 * VARIABLES USED: file_to_insert: pointer to file to insert.
 *                 second_file: pointer to the file being inserted
 *                              into.
 *                 output_file: destination of the output (file or
 *                              stdout).
 *                 string: line read from the file.
 *                 insert_location: line number to insert the file
 *                                  file at.
 *                 length_of_file: number of lines in the second file.
 *                 argc: number of command line arguments.
 *                 argv: array of pointers to the command line.
 *
 * PSEUDO CODE: if (enough command line arguments are not present)
 *                 print an error message
 *                 exit to the operating system
 *
 *              if (line number specified is invalid) -- not a number
 *                 print an error message
 *                 exit to the operating system
 *
 *              get the length of the second file
 *
 *              if (the location to insert at is > the length
 *                  of second file)
 *                assign insert_location the length of second file
 *                   and treat insert as an append
 *
 *              if (argc < 5)          -- no output file was specified
 *                assign output_file = stdout
 *
 *              if (the input and output files are the same)
 *                 print an error message
 *                 exit to the operating system -- most small
```

```
*                      operating systems will not allow us to open
*                      the same file twice
*
*              if (either of the files cannot be opened)
*                      print an error message
*                      exit to the operating system
*
*              invoke the routine file_insert() to insert the file
*                 into the second file
*
*              close the files
*
*/


#include <stdio.h>        /* contains definitions for file I/O */
#include "defn.h"
#include "strings.h"
#include "fwriteln.c"   /* contains the routine fwriteln() */
#include "intcvrt.c"    /* contains the routine int_convert() */
#include "filelen.c"    /* contains the routine file_line_count() */
#include "strequal.c"   /* contains the routine strings_are_equal() */

main (argc, argv)
  int argc;             /* number of command line arguments */
  char *argv[];         /* array of pointers to the command line */
  {
  FILE *file_to_insert;
  FILE *output_file;
  FILE *fopen ();
  FILE *second_file;            /* file being inserted into */

  char string[MAX_STRING];      /* string read from the file */

  int insert_location;          /* line number to insert the file at */
  int length_of_file;           /* length of the file inserted into */

  if (argc < 4)                 /* see if the file names are present */
    {
    printf ("insert: useage:  insert file_to_insert  ");
    printf ("line#  file2  [output_file]\n");
    exit (1);
    }

  /* get the line number to insert the file at */

  if (int_convert (argv[2], &insert_location) == IO_ERROR)
    {
    printf ("insert: invalid line number specified %s\n", argv[2]);
    exit (1);
    }

  /* get the length of the second file */

  if ((length_of_file = file_line_count (argv[3])) ==  ERROR)
    {
```

```
      printf ("insert: error opening file %s\n", argv[3]);
      exit (1);
    }

/* make sure that the insertion location is <= length of file to be
   inserted into */

else if (insert_location > length_of_file)
    insert_location = length_of_file + 1;    /* treat as an append */

  /* see if the files were successfully opened and, if so,
   * insert it at the line specified in the second file,
   * otherwise print an error message.
   */

if ((file_to_insert = fopen (argv[1], "r")) == NULL)
  {
    printf ("insert: error opening file %s\n", argv[1]);
    exit (1);
  }

if ((second_file = fopen (argv[3], "r")) == NULL)
  {
    printf ("insert: error opening file %s\n", argv[3]);
    exit (1);
  }

if (argc < 5)              /* insert line# file1 file2 */
  output_file = stdout;

/* insure that the input file is different from the output file */

else if (strings_are_equal (argv[4], argv[3]))
  {
    printf ("insert: output file must differ from input.\n");
    exit (1);
  }

else if (strings_are_equal (argv[4], argv[2]))
  {
    printf ("insert: output file must differ from input.\n");
    exit (1);
  }

else if ((output_file = fopen (argv[4], "w")) == NULL)
  {
    printf ("insert: error opening file %s.\n", argv[4]);
    exit (1);
  }

/* insert the file */

file_insert (file_to_insert, second_file, output_file,
            insert_location);

fclose (file_to_insert);
```

```
   fclose (second_file);

    if (argc == 5)        /* if an output file was opened close it */
      fclose (output_file);
   }




/*
 *  NAME: file_insert (file_to_insert, second_file, output_file,
 *                     insert_location)
 *
 *  FUNCTION: Inserts a file into a second file at the line
 *            number specified in insert_location.
 *
 *  VARIABLES USED: input_file: pointer to the file to insert.
 *                  second_file: pointer to the file inserted into.
 *                  output_file: pointer to the output file.
 *                  insert_location: line number to insert the
 *                                   file at.
 *
 *  ROUTINES CALLED: fwriteln (); writes a line to a file and
 *                               insures only one newline
 *                               character is written.
 *
 *  PSEUDO CODE: write the lines in the second file which
 *               precede the insertion location to the output
 *               file
 *
 *               write the lines contained in the file to insert
 *               to the output file
 *
 *               write the remainder of the second file to
 *               the output file
 *
 *               return -- the file is inserted
 *
 */


file_insert (file_to_insert, second_file, output_file,
             insert_location)

  FILE *file_to_insert;
  FILE *second_file;       /* file inserted into */
  FILE *output_file;

  int insert_location;   /* line number in the second file
                                 to insert at */
{
   int count;

   char string[MAX_STRING];  /* line read from a file */

    /* read and write the lines in second file
       which precede the insertion location */
```

```
    for (count = 1; count < insert_location; count++)

        {
          fgets (string, MAX_STRING, second_file);
          fwriteln (output_file, string);
        }

    /* insert the file */

    while (fgets (string, MAX_STRING, file_to_insert))
        fwriteln (output_file, string);

    /* write the remainder of the second file */

    while (fgets (string, MAX_STRING, second_file))
        fwriteln (output_file, string);
}
```

The Tab program inserts a tab at the beginning of each line of a file. When programs are developed with an editor or word processor, the code usually starts in column one. Unfortunately, if you later want to place the source code in a notebook containing other C utilities, holes cannot be placed in the papers without affecting the code. The Tab program eliminates this problem by allowing you pad each line with several blanks. The calling sequence for Tab is

```
        tab input_file [output_file]
```

```
/*
 * NAME: tab.c
 *
 * FUNCTION: Insert a series of blanks at the start of each line
 *           in a file.
 *
 * ROUTINES CALLED: tab_file(); places the blanks in front of each
 *                       line read and writes the line to an
 *                       output file or stdout.
 *                   pad_string(); called by tab_file() to pad the string
 *                       with the number of blanks specified.
 *
 * VARIABLES USED: file1, file2: pointers to the input file and output
 *                       destination (stdout or file).
 *                 argv: array of pointers to the command line.
 *                 argc: count of command line arguments.
 *
 * PSEUDO CODE: if (enough command line arguments are not present)
 *                  print an error message
 *                  exit to the operating system
 *
 *              if (only 2 command line arguments are specified)
 *                  assign output_file to stdout
 *                  (i.e. no output file was specified)
 *
```

```
*                   if (the input and output file names are the same)
*                           print an error message
*                           exit to the operating system -- most
*                           small operating systems will not
*                           allow us to open the same file twice
*
*                   if (either of the files cannot be opened)
*                     (stdout does not have to be opened)
*                     print an error message
*                     exit to the operating system
*
*                   invoke tab_file() to place the tabs in each line
*                           read from the file
*
*                   close the input file
*
*                   if (an output file was opened)
*                           close the output file
*
*/


#include <stdio.h>       /* definitions for file I/O */
#include "defn.h"
#include "fwriteln.c"     /* contains the routine fwriteln() */
#include "strpad.c"       /* contains the routine pad_string() */
#include "strappnd.c"     /* contains the routine append_string() */
#include "strequal.c"     /* contains the routine strings_are_equal() */
#include "strcopy.c"      /* contains the routine copy_string() */

#define TAB_SPACE 8       /* number of spaces to insert in a line */

main (argc, argv)
  int argc;               /* number of command line arguments */
  char *argv[];           /* array of pointers to the command line */
  {
  FILE *input_file;       /* input file to insert tabs into.*/
  FILE *output_file;      /* pointer to the optional output file */
  FILE *fopen ();

  if (argc < 2)           /* see if an input file name is present */
    {
    printf ("tab: no file specified\n");
    exit (1);
    }

  /* see if the files can be opened successfully and, if so, tab
   * the lines contained in the input file and print them either
   * to stdout or an output file. if either file cannot be opened
   * print an error message and exit to the operating system.
   */

  if ((input_file = fopen (argv[1], "r")) == NULL)
    {
    printf ("tab: error opening file %s\n", argv[1]);
    exit (1);
    }
```

```
   if (argc < 3)              /* tab file_name */
     output_file = stdout;

   /* make sure that the input file and output file are different */

   else if (strings_are_equal (argv[1], argv[2]))
    {
     printf ("tab: input and output files must differ\n");
     exit (1);
    }

   else if ((output_file = fopen (argv[2], "w")) == NULL)
    {
     printf ("tab: error opening file %s\n", argv[2]);
     exit (1);
    }

   tab_file (input_file, output_file);

   fclose (input_file);

   if (argc == 3)            /* if an output file was opened, close it */
     fclose (output_file);
}



/*
 * NAME: tab_file (input_file, output_file)
 *
 * FUNCTION: Inserts tabs into each line read from the  file
 *           specified, and writes the new line to the output
 *           file specified or stdout.
 *
 * EXAMPLE: tab_file (argv[1], argv[2]);
 *
 * VARIABLES USED: input_file: pointer to the input file.
 *                 output_file: pointer to the output file, or
 *                              stdout.
 *                 string: string read from the file.
 *
 * ROUTINES CALLED: pad_string (); inserts blanks in front of a string.
 *                  fwriteln (); writes a string to a file insuring that
 *                               only one newline character is written.
 *
 * PSEUDO CODE:  while (the input file contains lines)
 *                  get a string from the file
 *                  pad the string with blanks
 *                  write the string to the output file
 *
 *               return -- the tabs have been inserted
 *
 */

tab_file (input_file, output_file)
   FILE *input_file;
   FILE *output_file;
```

```
{
  char string [MAX_STRING];  /* buffer for the string read
                                from the input file */

  while (fgets (string, MAX_STRING, input_file))
    {
      pad_string (string, TAB_SPACE);
      fwriteln (output_file, string);
    }
}
```

C H A P T E R

Programming The Pipe

The *pipe* is a tool supported by UNIX and MS-DOS that allows you to direct the output of one program to become the input of a second program. For example, the command **DIRECTORY | SORT** directs the output of the DIRECTORY command to become the input of the SORT command.

Many of the routines in this book can be modified slightly to support the pipe. In Chapter 10, for instance, the input file specification was included as a command-line argument, **LINENUM SOMEFILE**. When you use the pipe, the input source (**stdin**) is directed by the operating system to point to the output of the previous program. Consider the following program:

```
#include <stdio.h>
#include "defn.h"

main ()
 {
  char string[MAX_STRING];   /* line read from stdin */

  int line_number = 1;        /* current line number */

  while (fgets(string, MAX_STRING, stdin))
    printf ("%d %s", line_number++, string);
 }
```

The program will read and output lines of input from **stdin** until an end-of-file (EOF) occurs. If you run the program without the pipe, the input lines will continue to echo until an EOF (CONTROL-D or Z on most systems) is entered. If you instead use the pipe to provide an input source, the output of the DIRECTORY command will be directed into the routine and each line will be provided with its line number.

For example, if the directory looks like this:

```
      Volume in drive B has no label
       Directory of B:\PREPLACE
  STRINGS   H     7808   1-01-80    1:45a
  STRINSRT  C     2688   2-17-84   12:24a
  DEFN      H      896   1-01-80    1:20a
  STRREMSS  C     2432   2-17-84   12:25a
  STREQUAL  C     1280   2-17-84   12:28a
  STRINDEX  C     1536   2-17-84   12:26a
  STRCOPY   C     1408   2-17-84   12:21a
  STRLEN    C     1152   2-17-84   12:20a
  PREPLACE  C     6528   1-01-80   12:22a
     11 File(s)      3072 bytes free
```

then the sequence **DIRECTORY | NUMBER** will output this version of the directory:

```
1
2    Volume in drive B has no label
3    Directory of B:\PREPLACE
4
5    .                <DIR>   1-01-80   12:04a
```

6	..		<DIR>	1-01-80	12:04a
7	STRINGS	H	7808	1-01-80	1:45a
8	STRINSRT	C	2688	2-17-84	12:24a
9	DEFN	H	896	1-01-80	1:20a
10	STRREMSS	C	2432	2-17-84	12:25a
11	STREQUAL	C	1280	2-17-84	12:28a
12	STRINDEX	C	1536	2-17-84	12:26a
13	STRCOPY	C	1408	2-17-84	12:21a
14	STRLEN	C	1152	2-17-84	12:20a
15	PREPLACE	C	6528	1-01-80	12:22a
16	11 File(s)		2048 bytes free		

It is interesting to note the difference in the number of free bytes remaining in the directory example. When the pipe is used on an MS-DOS system, two temporary files are opened. Although they do not show up in the directory listing, their presence is made evident by the amount of disk space consumed. In this example, each file required 512 bytes.

Modifying Applications To Support the Pipe

As stated earlier, when the output of one program is piped into another program, the operating system modifies the file pointers **stdout** and **stdin**.

To utilize the pipe, you must modify your routines to obtain their input from **stdin**:

```
while (fgets(string, MAX_STRING, stdin))
   {
   /* remainder of the code */
   }
```

When the first program completes, the value NULL is returned from **fgets( )** and the second program will terminate.

The following list provides the new command structure for the routines in this chapter. Each routine name has been preceded with a **p** (pipe) to distinguish it from the routines in Chapter 10.

PROGRAM | PCOMP FILENAME
PROGRAM | PSHOW
PROGRAM | PFIRST [n]
PROGRAM | PFINDWORD [-s] WORD
PROGRAM | PREPLACE -dq WORD [WORD]
PROGRAM | PDIFF [-s] FILENAME
PROGRAM | PCRYPT KEY [FILENAME]

It is important to note that you are not restricted to using the pipe only once in each command line. For example, the command **DIRECTORY | PFINDWORD .C | PSHOW** pipes the output of the DIRECTORY command into the routine **PFINDWORD**, which searches for .C. The output of **PFINDWORD** is then piped to **PSHOW**, which displays the names of all the files containing the .C notation a screenful at a time.

```
/*
 * NAME: pcomp.c
 *
 * FUNCTION: Returns the line number and character location of the
 *           first difference between a program output and a file.
 *
 * ROUTINES CALLED: string_comp(); returns the character location
 *                                 of the first difference in two
 *                                 strings, or -1 if the strings
 *                                 are equal.
 *
 * MACROS USED: NOT(); performs a Boolean NOT.
 *
 * VARIABLES USED: line_count: contains the current line number.
 *                 eop: TRUE if the end of the input program has occurred.
 *                 eof: TRUE if the end of the file has occurred.
 *                 location: character location of the first
 *                           difference.
 *                 done_with_comparison: TRUE or FALSE.
 *                 argv: array of pointers to the command line.
 *                 argc: number of command line arguments.
 *                 file: pointer to the file to compare.
 *                 string2: line read from stdin.
 *                 string1: line read from the file.
 *
 * PSEUDO CODE: initialize done_with_comparison to FALSE
 *              if (enough command line arguments are not present)
 *                print an error message
 *                exit to the operating system
 *
 *              if (the file cannot be opened)
 *                print an error message
 *                exit to the operating system
 *
```

```
*                 while (not_done_with_comparison)
*                    get a line from stdin
*                    get a line the from file
*
*                    if (the end of the file or program has occurred)
*                       the first difference is found
*                       print the location of the first difference
*
*                    else if (the end of both has occurred)
*                       the file and program output were identical
*
*                    else (both contained lines)
*                       if (the lines are different)
*                          the first difference is found
*                          print the location of the first difference
*
*                    if (the first difference was found OR
*                          the file and program output were identical)
*                       set done_with_comparison = TRUE
*
*                 close the file
*
*/

#include <stdio.h>      /* contains definitions for file I/O */
#include "defn.h"
#include "strings.h"
#include "math.h"
#include "strcomp.c"  /* contains the routine string_comp() */

main (argc, argv)
   int argc;           /* number of command line arguments */
   char *argv[];       /* array of pointers to the command line */
   {
   FILE *file;
   FILE *fopen();

   int line_count;           /* line number we are displaying */

   int location = -1;        /* location of the first difference */

   int eop = FALSE;          /* end of program input */
   int eof = FALSE;          /* end of file */

   int done_with_comparison = FALSE;

   char string2[MAX_STRING]; /* line read from the program output */
   char string1[MAX_STRING]; /* line read from the file */

   if (argc < 2)             /* see if the file name is present */
    {
     printf ("pcomp: invalid useage: pcomp file\n");
     exit (1);
    }
```

```
/* see if the file was successfully opened and, if so, display
 * the location of the first difference, otherwise print an
 * error message for the file we cannot open.
 */

if ((file = fopen (argv[1], "r")) == NULL)
  {
   printf ("pcomp: error opening the file %s\n", argv[1]);
   exit (1);
  }

/* examine the file and program output for the first difference */

for (line_count = 1; NOT(done_with_comparison); line_count++)
  {
     if (fgets (string1, MAX_STRING, file) == NULL)   /* end of file? */
        eof = TRUE;

     if (fgets (string2, MAX_STRING, stdin) == NULL) /* end of program? */
        eop = TRUE;

     if (eof && eop)  /* the file and program output were identical */
       break;

     if (eof || eop)  /* end of either the file or program input */
        {
           printf ("\npcomp: first difference is line %d character %d\n",
                   line_count, 0);

           done_with_comparison = TRUE;

           location = 0; /* we will test location to see if a difference */
                         /* was found. if location == -1 no difference */
                         /* was found. */
        }

     else if ((location = string_comp (string1, string2)) != -1)
        {
           printf ("\npcomp: first difference is line %d character %d\n",
                   line_count, location);

           done_with_comparison = TRUE;
        }
  }

if (location == -1)
   printf ("pcomp: program output and file are identical\n");

fclose (file);
}
```

_____

```
/*
 * NAME: pshow.c
 *
 * FUNCTION: Displays the output of a program to the screen one
 *           screenful at a time.
 *
 * ROUTINES CALLED: writeln(): writes a string to stdout insuring
 *                             that only one newline character is
 *                             written.
 *
 * VARIABLES USED: line_count: number of lines displayed.
 *                 argc: number of command line arguments.
 *                 argv: array of pointers to the command line.
 *                 string: line read from stdin.
 *
 * PSEUDO CODE: initialize the line count to 0
 *
 *              while (lines are input to stdin)
 *                 get a line
 *                 display the line to stdout
 *                 increment the line count
 *
 *                 if (a screenful has been displayed)
 *                    pause and prompt the user to hit <RETURN>
 *
 */

#include <stdio.h>            /* contains definitions for file I/O */
#include "defn.h"
#include "strings.h"

#include "writeln.c"          /* contains the routine writeln() */

#define DISPLAY_PAGE 22       /* number of lines to display before
                                 pausing with the display message */

 main (argc, argv)
   int argc;                  /* number of command line arguments */
   char *argv[];              /* array of pointers to the command line */
  {
   int line_count = 0;        /* line number we are displaying */

   char string[MAX_STRING]; /* line read from stdin */

   /* read a line from stdin and display it.

      once the number of lines displayed is equal to the
      display page, pause and ask the user to hit <RETURN>. */

   while (fgets (string, MAX_STRING, stdin))
     {
       writeln (string);  /* display the line */

       if (++line_count % DISPLAY_PAGE == 0)
         {
           printf ("Hit <RETURN> to continue\n");
```

```
        /* because the file pointer stdin has been redefined by the
           pipe, we will input the data from the user via the file
           pointer stderr which is defined to point to the console */

        while (getc(stderr) != EOL) /* read until the buffer is empty ⟩
            ;
    }
  }
}
```

```
/*
 * NAME: pfirst.c
 *
 * FUNCTION: Displays the number of lines specified in the command line
 *           starting with the first line input to stdin.  If no lines are
 *           specified, pfirst will display 10 lines by default.
 *
 * ROUTINES CALLED: int_convert(); converts a string to the corresponding
 *                              integer value.
 *                  display_command_line(); displays the command line
 *                              entered to invoke the program.
 *                  fwriteln(); writes a line to a file insuring that
 *                              only one newline character is written.
 *
 * VARIABLES USED: output_file: pointer to the output destination (file
 *                           or stdout).
 *                 lines_present: TRUE if the number of lines to
 *                           display is specified.
 *                 output_index: index into argv[] of the name of the
 *                           output file.
 *                 string: line read from stdin.
 *                 count: counter.
 *                 number_of_lines: number of lines to display.
 *
 * PSEUDO CODE: if (enough command line arguments are not present)
 *                  print an error message
 *                  exit to the operating system
 *
 *              if (argv[1] can be converted to an integer)
 *                  number of lines to print = int_convert(argv[1])
 *              else
 *                  number of lines to print = 10 by default
 *
 *              if (argc > 2) -- the number of lines to display
 *                              is present
 *
 *              if (the output file cannot be opened)
 *                 print an error message
 *                 exit to the operating system
 *
 *              if (argc < 2 or argc == 2 and the number of lines
 *                  to display is present)
 *                  output_file = stdout  (no output file specified)
 *
```

```
 *                initialize count to 0
 *                while (count < the number of lines to display AND
 *                       lines are input to stdin)
 *                  get a line from stdin
 *                  write it to the output destination
 *                  increment count
 *
 *                if (an output file was opened)
 *                  close the output file
 */
#include <stdio.h>      /* contains definitions for file I/O */
#include "defn.h"
#include "strings.h"
#include "fwriteln.c" /* contains the routine fwriteln() */
#include "intcvrt.c"  /* contains the routine int_convert() */
#include "echo.c"      /* contains the routine display_command_line() */

main (argc, argv)
  int argc;              /* number of command line arguments */
  char *argv[];          /* array of pointers to the command line */
{
  FILE *output_file;  /* file written to, or stdout */
  FILE *fopen();

  int count;                 /* counter */
  int number_of_lines = 10;  /* default value */

  int output_index = argc -1; /* location of the name of the output
                                  file in argv[] */

  int lines_present = FALSE;  /* TRUE if the user specified the
                                 number of lines to display */

  int opened_output_file = FALSE; /* was output to a file or stdout? */

  char string[MAX_STRING];        /* string read from stdin */

  if (argc >= 2)     /* see if the number of lines desired is present */

    if (int_convert (argv[1], &number_of_lines) == IO_ERROR)
       number_of_lines = 10;                 /* by default */

     else if (argc > 2)   /* pfirst # file */
       lines_present = TRUE;

     else    /* pfirst # */
        lines_present = TRUE;           /* number of lines specified by
                                           the user was valid */

  /* if no output file is specified, print to stdout */

  if (argc < 2)
    output_file = stdout;

  else if (argc == 2 && lines_present)
    output_file = stdout;
```

```
  else
    {
     if ((output_file = fopen (argv[output_index], "w")) == NULL)
       {
         printf ("pfirst: error opening file %s\n", argv[output_index]);
         display_command_line (argv);
         exit (1);
       }
     opened_output_file = TRUE;
    }

  for (count = 0; count < number_of_lines; count++)
    {
     if (fgets (string, MAX_STRING, stdin) == NULL)
        break;   /* end of file was encountered */
     else
        fwriteln (output_file, string);
    }

  if (opened_output_file) /* if the output is to stdout */
    fclose (output_file); /* don't close a file */
}
```

```
/*
 * NAME: pfindword.c
 *
 * FUNCTION: Displays the contents and line number of all lines in
 *           the program output which contain the word specified in the
 *           command line.
 *
 * ROUTINES CALLED: writeln(); writes a line to the stdout insuring
 *                            only one newline character is written.
 *                  str_index(); returns the starting location of
 *                            a substring within a string, or -1
 *                            if the substring did not exist.
 *
 * VARIABLES USED: line_number: current line number.
 *                 lines_displayed: number of lines displayed.
 *                 stop_scrolling: if TRUE, scrolling is suppressed,
 *                            otherwise lines will continue to
 *                            scoll.
 *                 word_index: index into argv[] containing
 *                            the word to find.
 *
 * PSEUDO CODE: if (enough command line arguments are not present)
 *                 print an error message (should be: pfindword word)
 *                 exit to the operating system
 *
 *              if (argc == 3)
 *                 if (the qualifier is valid)
 *                     suppress scrolling
 *                 else
```

```
*                       display an error message
*                       do not suppress scrolling
*
*               initialize the line number to 0
*
*               while (the input source provides lines)
*                  get a line from stdin
*                  increment the line number
*                  if (the line contains the word)
*                     print the line number and line
*                     increment the count of lines displayed
*
*                  if (scrolling supression is desired)
*                     if (a page has been displayed)
*                        pause and prompt for <RETURN>
*                        set lines displayed to 0
*
*/

#include <stdio.h>        /* contains definitions for file I/0 */
#include "defn.h"
#include "strings.h"
#include "writeln.c"      /* contains the routine writeln() */
#include "strindex.c"     /* contains the routine str_index() */

#define DISPLAY_PAGE 21 /* number of lines to display before

                            pausing if scrolling has been supressed */

main (argc, argv)
   int argc;              /* number of command line arguments */
   char *argv[];          /* array of pointers to the command line */
   {
   int line_number = 0;          /* line number we are displaying */

   int lines_displayed = 0;      /* number of lines we have displayed */
                                 /* on the current page */

   int stop_scrolling = FALSE; /* TRUE if user wants to suppress
                                   scrolling with each page */

   int word_index = argc - 1; /* location of the word in argv[] */

   char string[MAX_STRING];    /* line read from stdin */

   if (argc < 2)               /* see if the word is present */
    {
    printf ("pfindword: invalid useage: pfindword [-s] word\n");
    exit (1);
    }

   if (argc == 3)              /* see if the qualifier is valid */
    {
      if (str_index ("-s-S", argv[1]) == -1)
        {
```

```
            printf ("\npfindword: invalid qualifier %s use -s\n", argv[1]);
            printf ("scrolling will not be suppressed\n");
            printf ("Hit <RETURN> to continue\n");

            /* because stdin has been redirected via the pipe, we must use
               the file pointer stderr to obtain the user input */

            while (getc(stderr) != EOL) ;
        }
      else
         stop_scrolling = TRUE;
  }

/* find and display each occurrence of the word */

while (fgets (string, MAX_STRING, stdin))
  {
    line_number++;

    /* if the line contains the word, print the line
       number and the contents of the string */

    if (str_index (string, argv[word_index]) != -1)
      {
          printf ("\n%d:", line_number);
          writeln (string);
          lines_displayed += 2;  /* \n and string */

      }

    /* see if scrolling should be suppressed */

    if (lines_displayed > DISPLAY_PAGE  && stop_scrolling)
      {
          printf ("\nHit <RETURN> to continue\n");

          while (getc(stderr) != EOL) ;

          lines_displayed = 0;
      }
  }
}
```

```
/*
 * NAME: preplace.c
 *
 * FUNCTION: Deletes or replaces each occurrence of a word within
 *           the output of a program which is directed to preplace
 *           via the pipe.
 *
 * ROUTINES CALLED: str_index (); returns the starting location of
 *                              a substring within a string.
 *                  remove_substring (); removes a substring from
 *                                    a string.
 *
```

```
*                    insert_string(); inserts a substring into a
*                                    string at the location specified.
*
* VARIABLES USED: delete: TRUE if the word is to be deleted.
*                 replace: TRUE if the word is to be replaced.
*                 output_index: location of the name of the output
*                               file in the array argv[].
*                 output_file: pointer to the output file.
*                 location: location of the substring in the string.
*                 length: length of the substring.
*                 string: line read from stdin.
*                 argc: number of command line arguments.
*                 argv: array of pointers to the command line.
*
* PSEUDO CODE: if (enough command line arguments are not present)
*                  print an error message
*                  exit to the operating system
*
*              find out which qualifier was provided -d or -r
*
*              if (the qualifier == -r)
*                set replace to TRUE
*
*          --  the command line will contain the
*              following if the qualifier is -r
*
*              preplace -r word new_word [file]
*
*              else if (the qualifier == -d)
*                set delete to TRUE
*
*              if (the qualifier is invalid)
*                print an error message
*                exit to the operating system
*
*              if (the output file cannot be opened)
*                print an error message
*                exit to the operating system
*
*              if (no output file is specified)
*                output_file = stdout
*
*              get the length of the substring
*
*              while (the input file contains lines)
*                get a line from the input file
*                while (the line contains the substring)
*                    if (delete)
*                       remove the substring
*                    else
*                       remove the substring
*                       insert the new string
*
*              if (an output file was opened)
*                close the output file
*
*/
```

```
#include <stdio.h>      /* contains definitions for file I/0 */
#include "defn.h"
#include "strings.h"
#include "strindex.c" /* contains the routine str_index() */
#include "strlen.c"    /* contains the routine string_length() */
#include "strremss.c" /* contains the routine remove_substring() */
#include "strinsrt.c" /* contains the routine insert_string() */
#include "strcopy.c"  /* contains the routine string_copy() */

main (argc, argv)
  int argc;               /* number of command line arguments */
  char *argv[];           /* array of pointers to the command line */
 {
  FILE *fopen();
  FILE *output_file = NULL;      /* if it equals NULL at the end of the */
                                 /* program no output file was opened.  */
                                 /* if it is not equal to NULL we must  */
                                 /* close a file                        */

  int delete = FALSE;      /* TRUE if the user wants the word deleted  */
  int replace = FALSE;     /* TRUE if the user wants the word replaced */

  int output_index = argc - 1; /* location in argv[] of the file name */

  int location;                /* location of the substring in the string */
  int length;                  /* length of the substring */

  char string[MAX_STRING]; /* string read from stdin */

  /* see if enough command line arguments are present */

  if (argc < 3)
   {
    printf ("preplace error: preplace -dr word [word] [file]\n");
    exit (1);
   }

  /* see which qualifier is present (-d) delete or (-r) replace */

  if (str_index("-d-D", argv[1]) != -1)
   delete = TRUE;

  else if (str_index ("-r-R", argv[1]) != -1)
    replace = TRUE;

  else
   {
    printf ("preplace: error in qualifier use -d or -r\n");
    exit(1);
   }

  /* see if an output file is desired, or if the output
     should go to the standard output via stdout */

  if (delete && argc == 3)             /* preplace -d word */
    output_file = stdout;
```

```
  else if (replace && argc == 4)   /* preplace -r word word */
    output_file = stdout;

  else if ((output_file = fopen (argv[output_index], "w")) == NULL)
    {
      printf ("preplace: error opening file %s\n", argv[output_index]);
      exit(1);
    }

  /* get the length of the old string */

  length = string_length (argv[2]);

  /* modify the input */

  while (fgets (string, MAX_STRING, stdin))
    {
      /* while the string contains the substring, delete or
         replace it */

      while ((location = str_index (string, argv[2])) != -1)

        if (delete)
          remove_substring (string, location, length);

        else
          {
            /* remove the string we are replacing */
            remove_substring (string, location, length);

            /* insert the new string */
            insert_string (string, argv[3], location);
          }

      fputs (string, output_file); /* write the corrected string */
    }

  if (output_file != NULL)   /* if an output file was opened */
    fclose (output_file);    /* close it. no need to close stdout */

}
```

```
/*
 * NAME: pdiff.c
 *
 * FUNCTION: Compares a file to the output of a program and displays
 *           the lines and line numbers of the lines which differ.
 *
 * ROUTINES CALLED: writeln(); writes a line to stdout insuring that
 *                            only one newline character is written.
 *                  str_index(); returns the starting location of a
 *                            substring within a string.
 *                  str_equal(); returns TRUE if two strings are equal,
 *                            otherwise FALSE is returned.
```

```
*
* MACROS USED: NOT(); performs a Boolean NOT.
*
* VARIABLES USED: file: pointer to the file to compare.
*                 line_count: contains the current line number.
*                 lines_displayed: contains the number of lines
*                                   that have been displayed.
*                 stop_scrolling: TRUE if scrolling is suppressed.
*                 eof: TRUE if the end of file has occurred.
*                 eop: TRUE if the end of the input program has occurred.
*                 done_with_file_comparison: TRUE or FALSE.
*                 string1: line read from the file.
*                 string2: line read from stdin.
*                 argv: array of pointers to the command line.
*                 argc: number of command line arguments.
*                 file_index: index to the file name in argv[].
*
* PSEUDO CODE: if (enough command line arguments are not present)
*                  print an error message
*                  exit to the operating system
*
*              if (the value in argc == 3)  --  pdiff -s file
*                  if (if qualifier is not valid)
*                      print an error message
*                      do not suppress scrolling
*                  else
*                      suppress scrolling
*
*              if (the file cannot be opened)
*                  print an error message
*                  exit to the operating system
*
*              initialize line_count to 0
*              initialize lines_displayed to 0
*
*              while (NOT done_with_file_comparison)
*                  if (the end of file has not occurred)
*                  get a line from the file
*
*                  if (the end of the program has not occurred)
*                  get a line from stdin
*
*                  if (either the file or program has reached
*                      the end of data)
*                      display the line_count, and line the read
*                        from the other since it is different
*                      increment the count of lines_displayed
*
*                  else if (both have reached the end of data)
*                      set done_with_file_comparison to TRUE
*
*                  else if (the strings are not equal)
*                      print the line_count and both strings
*                      increment the count of lines_displayed
*
```

```
 *                 if (suppress scrolling is desired)
 *                    if (a screenful of lines has been written)
 *                       prompt the user to hit <RETURN>
 *                       set lines_displayed to 0
 *
 *                 increment line_count
 *
 *              close the file
 *
 */

#include <stdio.h>      /* contains definitions for file I/O */
#include "defn.h"
#include "math.h"
#include "strings.h"
#include "writeln.c"   /* contains the routine writeln() */
#include "strindex.c"  /* contains the routine str_index() */
#include "strequal.c"  /* contains the routine strings_are_equal() */

#define DISPLAY_PAGE 20  /* number of lines to display before
                             pausing for the user to hit <return> */

main (argc, argv)
  int argc;          /* number of command line arguments */
  char *argv[];      /* array of pointers to the command line entered */
  {
  FILE *file;        /* file specified in command line to compare
                        to the program output */
  FILE *fopen ();

  int line_count;              /* line number we are displaying */
  int lines_displayed = 0; /* number of lines we've displayed */
                               /* on the current page */

  int file_index = argc - 1;   /* location in the array argv[] of the
                                  name of the file */

  int stop_scrolling = FALSE;  /* TRUE if the -s qualifier is present */

  int eof = FALSE;              /* end of file */
  int eop = FALSE;              /* end of input program */

  int done_with_file_comparison = FALSE;

  char string1[MAX_STRING];    /* line read from the file */
  char string2[MAX_STRING];    /* line read from stdin */

  if (argc < 2)                /* see if a file name is present */
    {
    printf ("pdiff: invalid useage: pdiff [-s] file\n");
    exit (1);
    }

  /* see if the qualifier -s was provided to suppress scrolling */

  if (argc == 3)  /* pdiff -x file */
    {
```

```
main (argc, argv)
   int argc;        /* number of command line arguments */
   char *argv[];    /* array of pointers to the command line entered */
{
  FILE *file;       /* file specified in command line to compare to program */
  FILE *fopen ();

  int line_count;            /* line number we are displaying */
  int lines_displayed = 0;   /* number of lines we've displayed */
                             /* on this screenful */

  int file_index = 1;        /* location in the array argv[] of the
                                name of the file */
                             /* if user specifies -s the file name
                                will be offset one location in argv[] */

  int stop_scrolling = FALSE;  /* TRUE if the -s qualifier is present */

  int eof = FALSE;        /* end of file */
  int eop = FALSE;        /* end of input program */

  int done_with_file_comparison = FALSE;

  char string1[MAX_STRING]; /* line read from file */
  char string2[MAX_STRING]; /* line read from stdin */

  if (argc < 2)          /* see if the file names are present */
   {
    printf ("pdiff: invalid useage: pdiff [-s] file\n");
    exit (1);
   }


  /* see if the qualifier -s was provided to suppress scrolling */

  if (argc == 3)   /* pdiff -x file file */
   {
    if (str_index ("-S-s", argv[1]) == -1)
      {
        printf ("pdiff: invalid qualifier %s use -s\n", argv[1]);
        printf ("pdiff: scrolling will not be suppressed\n");
        printf ("pdiff: hit <return> to continue\n");

        /* because the file pointer stdin has been modified via the
           pipe, we must use the file pointer stderr to obtain the
           user input */

        while (getc(stderr) != EOL) ;
      }

    else
      stop_scrolling = TRUE;  /* user wants scrolling suppressed */

    file_index++;   /* increment the index into argv[] of each file */
   }
```

```
    if (str_index ("-S-s", argv[1]) == -1)
      {
      printf ("pdiff: invalid qualifier %s use -s\n", argv[1]);
      printf ("pdiff: scrolling will not be suppressed\n");
      printf ("pdiff: hit <return> to continue\n");

      /* because the file pointer stdin has been modified via the
         pipe, we must use the file pointer stderr to obtain the
         user input */

      while (getc(stderr) != EOL) ;
      }

    else
      stop_scrolling = TRUE;      /* user wants scrolling suppressed */
    }

/* see if the file was successfully opened and, if so, display
 * the differences, otherwise print an error message.
 */

if ((file = fopen (argv[file_index], "r")) == NULL)
  {
  printf ("pdiff: error opening the file %s\n", argv[file_index]);
  exit (1);
  }

/* find and display any differences along with the line number */

for (line_count = 1; NOT(done_with_file_comparison); line_count++)
  {
    /* test for the end of file */

    if (NOT(eof))
      if (fgets (string1, MAX_STRING, file) == NULL)
        eof = TRUE;

    /* test for the end of program input */

    if (NOT(eop))
      if (fgets (string2, MAX_STRING, stdin) == NULL)
        eop = TRUE;

    if (NOT(eof) && NOT(eop))  /* compare the strings */
      {
      if (strings_are_equal (string1, string2) == FALSE)
        {
        printf ("\n%s: %d: ", argv[file_index], line_count);
        writeln (string1);

        printf ("stdin: %d: ", line_count);
        writeln (string2);

        lines_displayed +=3;  /* for the display page count */
        }
      }
```

```
        else if (NOT(eof))
          {
              printf ("\n%s: %d: ", argv[file_index], line_count);
              writeln (string1);
              lines_displayed++;
          }

        else if (NOT(eop))
          {
              printf ("\nstdin: %d: ", line_count);
              writeln (string2);
              lines_displayed++;
          }

        else
          done_with_file_comparison = TRUE;


/* if the user has entered the stop_scroll qualifier (-s), we want
 * to stop the output after each page is displayed.  since the number
 * of lines displayed gets incremented by 3 in one instance and 1 in
 * others, the mod operator (%) will not work (i.e. lines_diplayed % 20)
 * For example,
 * if seven lines in a row are different, lines_displayed will equal 21
 * so the test lines_displayed % 20 fails and the output will continue
 * to scroll.  therefore, we will keep a count of the number of lines
 * we have displayed on this page.  once this count is > DISPLAY_PAGE
 * we will prompt the user for a return and reset the count for the next
 * page.
 */

        if ((lines_displayed > DISPLAY_PAGE) && (stop_scrolling))
          {
            printf ("\nHit <RETURN> to continue\n");

            while (getc(stderr) != EOL) ;

            lines_displayed = 0;
          }




        }

      fclose (file);
    }
```

```
/*
 * NAME: pcrypt.c
 *
 * FUNCTION: Encrypts or decrypts a file with the key passed to
 *           it in the command line.
 *
 *
```

```
 * ROUTINES CALLED: strings_are_equal(); returns TRUE if two strings
 *                                    are equal, otherwise FALSE
 *                                    is returned.
 *                   crypt(): encrypts or decrypts the file it receives
 *               .                based upon the key provided.
 *                   copy_string(): copies the first character string to
 *                                    the second string provided.
 *
 * VARIABLES USED: output_file: pointer to the output file.
 *                 argv: array of pointers to the command line.
 *                 argc: number of command line arguments.
 *
 * PSEUDO CODE: if (enough command line arguments are not present)
 *                 print an error message (pcrypt key [file])
 *                 exit to the operating system
 *
 *              if (the output file cannot be opened)
 *                 print an error message
 *                 exit to the operating system
 *
 *              while (data is piped to the program)
 *                get and encrypt a character
 *                write the character to the output destination
 *
 *              if (an output file was opened)
 *                close the file
 *
 */

#include <stdio.h>      /* contains definitions for file I/O */
#include "defn.h"
#include "strings.h"
#include "math.h"
#include "fwriteln.c" /* contains the routine fwriteln() */
#include "strlen.c"   /* contains the routine string_length() */
#include "strequal.c" /* contains the routine strings_are_equal() */
#include "strcopy.c"  /* contains the routine string_copy() */

main (argc, argv)
  int argc;              /* number of command line arguments */
  char *argv[];          /* array of pointers to the command line */
{
  FILE *output_file;
  FILE *fopen ();

  int i = 0;
  int key_length;
  int letter;

  char key[MAX_STRING];     /* encryption key */

  if (argc < 2)             /* see if the key is present */
  {
    printf ("pcrypt: invalid useage: pcrypt key [file]\n");
    exit (1);
  }

  if (argc < 3)             /* pcrypt key [file] */
    output_file = stdout;   /* no output file was specified */
```

```
else
  if ((output_file = fopen (argv[2], "w")) == NULL)
    {
      printf ("pcrypt: error opening file %s\n", argv[2]);
      exit (1);
    }

copy_string (argv[1], key);

key_length = string_length (key);  /* get the length of the key */

while ((letter = getc(stdin)) != EOF)
  {
    if (NOT(is_control(letter)))
      {
        letter = XOR(letter, (key[i %  key_length]));
```

/* we will test to insure the result of the XOR is not a control
   character. if it is, we will convert it back to the original
   character. this is because a control z represents an end of
   file. if we write this value, the program which decrypts the
   file will think it has found the end of file due to the control
   z. since control characters do not appear often in a file,
   converting the character back to their original values
   does not affect the encrypted result. likewise, when we later
   decrypt the file, the correct letter is obtained since it is
   first converted to a control character, and then back to its
   original value.
*/

```
        if (is_control(letter))
          letter = XOR(letter, (key[i %  key_length]));

        putc(letter, output_file);

        i++;
      }
    else
      putc(letter, output_file);

  }

if (argc == 3)              /* if the output was directed to stdout */
  fclose (output_file); /* don't close a file */
}
```

A P P E N D I X ·

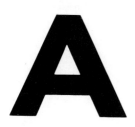

ASCII Codes

Table A-1 lists the ASCII codes for characters.

Table A-1.   *ASCII Character Codes*

DEC	OCTAL	HEX	ASCII		DEC	OCTAL	HEX	ASCII
0	000	00	NUL		10	012	0A	LF
1	001	01	SOH		11	013	0B	VT
2	002	02	STX		12	014	0C	FF
3	003	03	ETX		13	015	0D	CR
4	004	04	EOT		14	016	0E	SO
5	005	05	ENQ		15	017	0F	SI
6	006	06	ACK		16	020	10	DLE
7	007	07	BEL		17	021	11	DC1
8	010	08	BS		18	022	12	DC2
9	011	09	HT		19	023	13	DC3

Table A-1. *ASCII Character Codes (continued)*

DEC	OCTAL	HEX	ASCII	DEC	OCTAL	HEX	ASCII
20	024	14	DC4	64	100	40	@
21	025	15	NAK	65	101	41	A
22	026	16	SYN	66	102	42	B
23	027	17	ETB	67	103	43	C
24	030	18	CAN	68	104	44	D
25	031	19	EM	69	105	45	E
26	032	1A	SUB	70	106	46	F
27	033	1B	ESC	71	107	47	G
28	034	1C	FS	72	110	48	H
29	035	1D	GS	73	111	49	I
30	036	1E	RS	74	112	4A	J
31	037	1F	US	75	113	4B	K
32	040	20	SPACE	76	114	4C	L
33	041	21	!	77	115	4D	M
34	042	22	"	78	116	4E	N
35	043	23	#	79	117	4F	O
36	044	24	$	80	120	50	P
37	045	25	%	81	121	51	Q
38	046	26	&	82	122	52	R
39	047	27	'	83	123	53	S
40	050	28	(	84	124	54	T
41	051	29	)	85	125	55	U
42	052	2A	*	86	126	56	V
43	053	2B	+	87	127	57	W
44	054	2C	,	88	130	58	X
45	055	2D	—	89	131	59	Y
46	056	2E	.	90	132	5A	Z
47	057	2F	/	91	133	5B	[
48	060	30	0	92	134	5C	\
49	061	31	1	93	135	5D	]
50	062	32	2	94	136	5E	^
51	063	33	3	95	137	5F	—
52	064	34	4	96	140	60	`
53	065	35	5	97	141	61	a
54	066	36	6	98	142	62	b
55	067	37	7	99	143	63	c
56	070	38	8	100	144	64	d
57	071	39	9	101	145	65	e
58	072	3A	:	102	146	66	f
59	073	3B	;	103	147	67	g
60	074	3C	<	104	150	68	h
61	075	3D	=	105	151	69	i
62	076	3E	>	106	152	6A	j
63	077	3F	?	107	153	6B	k

Table A-1. *ASCII Character Codes (continued)*

DEC	OCTAL	HEX	ASCII		DEC	OCTAL	HEX	ASCII
108	154	6C	l		118	166	76	v
109	155	6D	m		119	167	77	w
110	156	6E	n		120	170	78	x
111	157	6F	o		121	171	79	y
112	160	70	p		122	172	7A	z
113	161	71	q		123	173	7B	{
114	162	72	r		124	174	7C	|
115	163	73	s		125	175	7D	}
116	164	74	t		126	176	7E	~
117	165	75	u		127	177	7F	DEL

Index